Mometrix
TEST PREPARATION

I0889393

Secrets of the

CPIM®

Detailed Scheduling and Planning Exam

Study Guide

DEAR FUTURE EXAM SUCCESS STORY

First of all, **THANK YOU** for purchasing Mometrix study materials!

Second, congratulations! You are one of the few determined test-takers who are committed to doing whatever it takes to excel on your exam. **You have come to the right place.** We developed these study materials with one goal in mind: to deliver you the information you need in a format that's concise and easy to use.

In addition to optimizing your guide for the content of the test, we've outlined our recommended steps for breaking down the preparation process into small, attainable goals so you can make sure you stay on track.

We've also analyzed the entire test-taking process, identifying the most common pitfalls and showing how you can overcome them and be ready for any curveball the test throws you.

Standardized testing is one of the biggest obstacles on your road to success, which only increases the importance of doing well in the high-pressure, high-stakes environment of test day. Your results on this test could have a significant impact on your future, and this guide provides the information and practical advice to help you achieve your full potential on test day.

Your success is our success

We would love to hear from you! If you would like to share the story of your exam success or if you have any questions or comments in regard to our products, please contact us at **800-673-8175** or **support@mometrix.com**.

Thanks again for your business and we wish you continued success!

Sincerely,
The Mometrix Test Preparation Team

Need more help? Check out our flashcards at:
http://MometrixFlashcards.com/CPIM

Written and edited by the Mometrix Exam Secrets Test Prep Team
Printed in the United States of America

TABLE OF CONTENTS

Introduction

Thank you for purchasing this resource! You have made the choice to prepare yourself for a test that could have a huge impact on your future, and this guide is designed to help you be fully ready for test day. Obviously, it's important to have a solid understanding of the test material, but you also need to be prepared for the unique environment and stressors of the test, so that you can perform to the best of your abilities.

For this purpose, the first section that appears in this guide is the **Secret Keys**. We've devoted countless hours to meticulously researching what works and what doesn't, and we've boiled down our findings to the five most impactful steps you can take to improve your performance on the test. We start at the beginning with study planning and move through the preparation process, all the way to the testing strategies that will help you get the most out of what you know when you're finally sitting in front of the test.

We recommend that you start preparing for your test as far in advance as possible. However, if you've bought this guide as a last-minute study resource and only have a few days before your test, we recommend that you skip over the first two Secret Keys since they address a long-term study plan.

If you struggle with **test anxiety**, we strongly encourage you to check out our recommendations for how you can overcome it. Test anxiety is a formidable foe, but it can be beaten, and we want to make sure you have the tools you need to defeat it.

Secret Key #1 – Plan Big, Study Small

There's a lot riding on your performance. If you want to ace this test, you're going to need to keep your skills sharp and the material fresh in your mind. You need a plan that lets you review everything you need to know while still fitting in your schedule. We'll break this strategy down into three categories.

Information Organization

Start with the information you already have: the official test outline. From this, you can make a complete list of all the concepts you need to cover before the test. Organize these concepts into groups that can be studied together, and create a list of any related vocabulary you need to learn so you can brush up on any difficult terms. You'll want to keep this vocabulary list handy once you actually start studying since you may need to add to it along the way.

Time Management

Once you have your set of study concepts, decide how to spread them out over the time you have left before the test. Break your study plan into small, clear goals so you have a manageable task for each day and know exactly what you're doing. Then just focus on one small step at a time. When you manage your time this way, you don't need to spend hours at a time studying. Studying a small block of content for a short period each day helps you retain information better and avoid stressing over how much you have left to do. You can relax knowing that you have a plan to cover everything in time. In order for this strategy to be effective though, you have to start studying early and stick to your schedule. Avoid the exhaustion and futility that comes from last-minute cramming!

Study Environment

The environment you study in has a big impact on your learning. Studying in a coffee shop, while probably more enjoyable, is not likely to be as fruitful as studying in a quiet room. It's important to keep distractions to a minimum. You're only planning to study for a short block of time, so make the most of it. Don't pause to check your phone or get up to find a snack. It's also important to **avoid multitasking**. Research has consistently shown that multitasking will make your studying dramatically less effective. Your study area should also be comfortable and well-lit so you don't have the distraction of straining your eyes or sitting on an uncomfortable chair.

The time of day you study is also important. You want to be rested and alert. Don't wait until just before bedtime. Study when you'll be most likely to comprehend and remember. Even better, if you know what time of day your test will be, set that time aside for study. That way your brain will be used to working on that subject at that specific time and you'll have a better chance of recalling information.

Finally, it can be helpful to team up with others who are studying for the same test. Your actual studying should be done in as isolated an environment as possible, but the work of organizing the information and setting up the study plan can be divided up. In between study sessions, you can discuss with your teammates the concepts that you're all studying and quiz each other on the details. Just be sure that your teammates are as serious about the test as you are. If you find that your study time is being replaced with social time, you might need to find a new team.

Secret Key #2 – Make Your Studying Count

You're devoting a lot of time and effort to preparing for this test, so you want to be absolutely certain it will pay off. This means doing more than just reading the content and hoping you can remember it on test day. It's important to make every minute of study count. There are two main areas you can focus on to make your studying count.

Retention

It doesn't matter how much time you study if you can't remember the material. You need to make sure you are retaining the concepts. To check your retention of the information you're learning, try recalling it at later times with minimal prompting. Try carrying around flashcards and glance at one or two from time to time or ask a friend who's also studying for the test to quiz you.

To enhance your retention, look for ways to put the information into practice so that you can apply it rather than simply recalling it. If you're using the information in practical ways, it will be much easier to remember. Similarly, it helps to solidify a concept in your mind if you're not only reading it to yourself but also explaining it to someone else. Ask a friend to let you teach them about a concept you're a little shaky on (or speak aloud to an imaginary audience if necessary). As you try to summarize, define, give examples, and answer your friend's questions, you'll understand the concepts better and they will stay with you longer. Finally, step back for a big picture view and ask yourself how each piece of information fits with the whole subject. When you link the different concepts together and see them working together as a whole, it's easier to remember the individual components.

Finally, practice showing your work on any multi-step problems, even if you're just studying. Writing out each step you take to solve a problem will help solidify the process in your mind, and you'll be more likely to remember it during the test.

Modality

Modality simply refers to the means or method by which you study. Choosing a study modality that fits your own individual learning style is crucial. No two people learn best in exactly the same way, so it's important to know your strengths and use them to your advantage.

For example, if you learn best by visualization, focus on visualizing a concept in your mind and draw an image or a diagram. Try color-coding your notes, illustrating them, or creating symbols that will trigger your mind to recall a learned concept. If you learn best by hearing or discussing information, find a study partner who learns the same way or read aloud to yourself. Think about how to put the information in your own words. Imagine that you are giving a lecture on the topic and record yourself so you can listen to it later.

For any learning style, flashcards can be helpful. Organize the information so you can take advantage of spare moments to review. Underline key words or phrases. Use different colors for different categories. Mnemonic devices (such as creating a short list in which every item starts with the same letter) can also help with retention. Find what works best for you and use it to store the information in your mind most effectively and easily.

Secret Key #3 – Practice the Right Way

Your success on test day depends not only on how many hours you put into preparing, but also on whether you prepared the right way. It's good to check along the way to see if your studying is paying off. One of the most effective ways to do this is by taking practice tests to evaluate your progress. Practice tests are useful because they show exactly where you need to improve. Every time you take a practice test, pay special attention to these three groups of questions:

- The questions you got wrong
- The questions you had to guess on, even if you guessed right
- The questions you found difficult or slow to work through

This will show you exactly what your weak areas are, and where you need to devote more study time. Ask yourself why each of these questions gave you trouble. Was it because you didn't understand the material? Was it because you didn't remember the vocabulary? Do you need more repetitions on this type of question to build speed and confidence? Dig into those questions and figure out how you can strengthen your weak areas as you go back to review the material.

Additionally, many practice tests have a section explaining the answer choices. It can be tempting to read the explanation and think that you now have a good understanding of the concept. However, an explanation likely only covers part of the question's broader context. Even if the explanation makes perfect sense, **go back and investigate** every concept related to the question until you're positive you have a thorough understanding.

As you go along, keep in mind that the practice test is just that: practice. Memorizing these questions and answers will not be very helpful on the actual test because it is unlikely to have any of the same exact questions. If you only know the right answers to the sample questions, you won't be prepared for the real thing. **Study the concepts** until you understand them fully, and then you'll be able to answer any question that shows up on the test.

It's important to wait on the practice tests until you're ready. If you take a test on your first day of study, you may be overwhelmed by the amount of material covered and how much you need to learn. Work up to it gradually.

On test day, you'll need to be prepared for answering questions, managing your time, and using the test-taking strategies you've learned. It's a lot to balance, like a mental marathon that will have a big impact on your future. Like training for a marathon, you'll need to start slowly and work your way up. When test day arrives, you'll be ready.

Start with the strategies you've read in the first two Secret Keys—plan your course and study in the way that works best for you. If you have time, consider using multiple study resources to get different approaches to the same concepts. It can be helpful to see difficult concepts from more than one angle. Then find a good source for practice tests. Many times, the test website will suggest potential study resources or provide sample tests.

Practice Test Strategy

If you're able to find at least three practice tests, we recommend this strategy:

Untimed and Open-Book Practice

Take the first test with no time constraints and with your notes and study guide handy. Take your time and focus on applying the strategies you've learned.

Timed and Open-Book Practice

Take the second practice test open-book as well, but set a timer and practice pacing yourself to finish in time.

Timed and Closed-Book Practice

Take any other practice tests as if it were test day. Set a timer and put away your study materials. Sit at a table or desk in a quiet room, imagine yourself at the testing center, and answer questions as quickly and accurately as possible.

Keep repeating timed and closed-book tests on a regular basis until you run out of practice tests or it's time for the actual test. Your mind will be ready for the schedule and stress of test day, and you'll be able to focus on recalling the material you've learned.

Secret Key #4 – Pace Yourself

Once you're fully prepared for the material on the test, your biggest challenge on test day will be managing your time. Just knowing that the clock is ticking can make you panic even if you have plenty of time left. Work on pacing yourself so you can build confidence against the time constraints of the exam. Pacing is a difficult skill to master, especially in a high-pressure environment, so **practice is vital**.

Set time expectations for your pace based on how much time is available. For example, if a section has 60 questions and the time limit is 30 minutes, you know you have to average 30 seconds or less per question in order to answer them all. Although 30 seconds is the hard limit, set 25 seconds per question as your goal, so you reserve extra time to spend on harder questions. When you budget extra time for the harder questions, you no longer have any reason to stress when those questions take longer to answer.

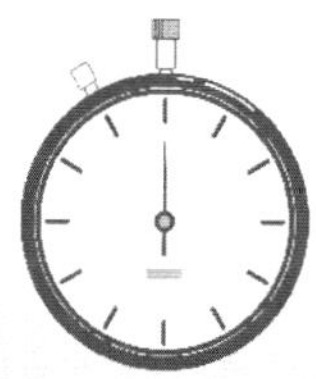

Don't let this time expectation distract you from working through the test at a calm, steady pace, but keep it in mind so you don't spend too much time on any one question. Recognize that taking extra time on one question you don't understand may keep you from answering two that you do understand later in the test. If your time limit for a question is up and you're still not sure of the answer, mark it and move on, and come back to it later if the time and the test format allow. If the testing format doesn't allow you to return to earlier questions, just make an educated guess; then put it out of your mind and move on.

On the easier questions, be careful not to rush. It may seem wise to hurry through them so you have more time for the challenging ones, but it's not worth missing one if you know the concept and just didn't take the time to read the question fully. Work efficiently but make sure you understand the question and have looked at all of the answer choices, since more than one may seem right at first.

Even if you're paying attention to the time, you may find yourself a little behind at some point. You should speed up to get back on track, but do so wisely. Don't panic; just take a few seconds less on each question until you're caught up. Don't guess without thinking, but do look through the answer choices and eliminate any you know are wrong. If you can get down to two choices, it is often worthwhile to guess from those. Once you've chosen an answer, move on and don't dwell on any that you skipped or had to hurry through. If a question was taking too long, chances are it was one of the harder ones, so you weren't as likely to get it right anyway.

On the other hand, if you find yourself getting ahead of schedule, it may be beneficial to slow down a little. The more quickly you work, the more likely you are to make a careless mistake that will affect your score. You've budgeted time for each question, so don't be afraid to spend that time. Practice an efficient but careful pace to get the most out of the time you have.

Secret Key #5 – Have a Plan for Guessing

When you're taking the test, you may find yourself stuck on a question. Some of the answer choices seem better than others, but you don't see the one answer choice that is obviously correct. What do you do?

The scenario described above is very common, yet most test takers have not effectively prepared for it. Developing and practicing a plan for guessing may be one of the single most effective uses of your time as you get ready for the exam.

In developing your plan for guessing, there are three questions to address:

- When should you start the guessing process?
- How should you narrow down the choices?
- Which answer should you choose?

When to Start the Guessing Process

Unless your plan for guessing is to select C every time (which, despite its merits, is not what we recommend), you need to leave yourself enough time to apply your answer elimination strategies. Since you have a limited amount of time for each question, that means that if you're going to give yourself the best shot at guessing correctly, you have to decide quickly whether or not you will guess.

Of course, the best-case scenario is that you don't have to guess at all, so first, see if you can answer the question based on your knowledge of the subject and basic reasoning skills. Focus on the key words in the question and try to jog your memory of related topics. Give yourself a chance to bring the knowledge to mind, but once you realize that you don't have (or you can't access) the knowledge you need to answer the question, it's time to start the guessing process.

It's almost always better to start the guessing process too early than too late. It only takes a few seconds to remember something and answer the question from knowledge. Carefully eliminating wrong answer choices takes longer. Plus, going through the process of eliminating answer choices can actually help jog your memory.

Summary: Start the guessing process as soon as you decide that you can't answer the question based on your knowledge.

How to Narrow Down the Choices

The next chapter in this book (**Test-Taking Strategies**) includes a wide range of strategies for how to approach questions and how to look for answer choices to eliminate. You will definitely want to read those carefully, practice them, and figure out which ones work best for you. Here though, we're going to address a mindset rather than a particular strategy.

Your odds of guessing an answer correctly depend on how many options you are choosing from.

Number of options left	5	4	3	2	1
Odds of guessing correctly	20%	25%	33%	50%	100%

You can see from this chart just how valuable it is to be able to eliminate incorrect answers and make an educated guess, but there are two things that many test takers do that cause them to miss out on the benefits of guessing:

- Accidentally eliminating the correct answer
- Selecting an answer based on an impression

We'll look at the first one here, and the second one in the next section.

To avoid accidentally eliminating the correct answer, we recommend a thought exercise called **the $5 challenge**. In this challenge, you only eliminate an answer choice from contention if you are willing to bet $5 on it being wrong. Why $5? Five dollars is a small but not insignificant amount of money. It's an amount you could afford to lose but wouldn't want to throw away. And while losing $5 once might not hurt too much, doing it twenty times will set you back $100. In the same way, each small decision you make—eliminating a choice here, guessing on a question there—won't by itself impact your score very much, but when you put them all together, they can make a big difference. By holding each answer choice elimination decision to a higher standard, you can reduce the risk of accidentally eliminating the correct answer.

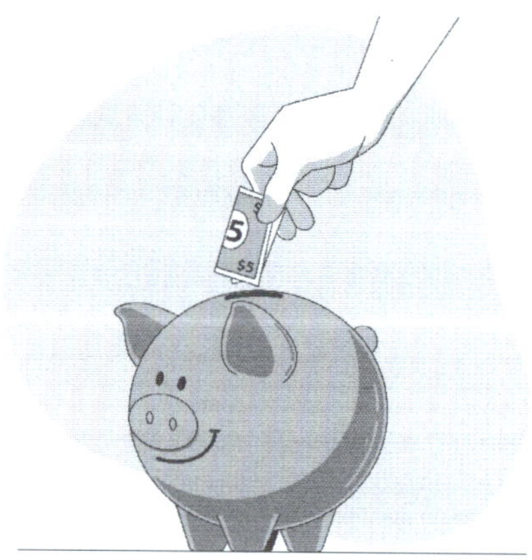

The $5 challenge can also be applied in a positive sense: If you are willing to bet $5 that an answer choice *is* correct, go ahead and mark it as correct.

Summary: Only eliminate an answer choice if you are willing to bet $5 that it is wrong.

Which Answer to Choose

You're taking the test. You've run into a hard question and decided you'll have to guess. You've eliminated all the answer choices you're willing to bet $5 on. Now you have to pick an answer. Why do we even need to talk about this? Why can't you just pick whichever one you feel like when the time comes?

The answer to these questions is that if you don't come into the test with a plan, you'll rely on your impression to select an answer choice, and if you do that, you risk falling into a trap. The test writers know that everyone who takes their test will be guessing on some of the questions, so they intentionally write wrong answer choices to seem plausible. You still have to pick an answer though, and if the wrong answer choices are designed to look right, how can you ever be sure that you're not falling for their trap? The best solution we've found to this dilemma is to take the decision out of your hands entirely. Here is the process we recommend:

Once you've eliminated any choices that you are confident (willing to bet $5) are wrong, select the first remaining choice as your answer.

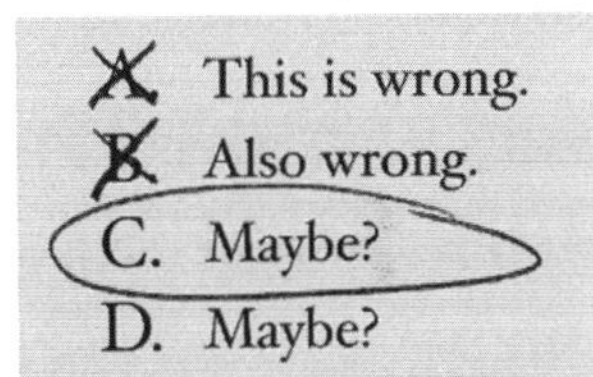

Whether you choose to select the first remaining choice, the second, or the last, the important thing is that you use some preselected standard. Using this approach guarantees that you will not be enticed into selecting an answer choice that looks right, because you are not basing your decision on how the answer choices look.

This is not meant to make you question your knowledge. Instead, it is to help you recognize the difference between your knowledge and your impressions. There's a huge difference between thinking an answer is right because of what you know, and thinking an answer is right because it looks or sounds like it should be right.

Summary: To ensure that your selection is appropriately random, make a predetermined selection from among all answer choices you have not eliminated.

Test-Taking Strategies

This section contains a list of test-taking strategies that you may find helpful as you work through the test. By taking what you know and applying logical thought, you can maximize your chances of answering any question correctly!

It is very important to realize that every question is different and every person is different: no single strategy will work on every question, and no single strategy will work for every person. That's why we've included all of them here, so you can try them out and determine which ones work best for different types of questions and which ones work best for you.

Question Strategies

☑ Read Carefully

Read the question and the answer choices carefully. Don't miss the question because you misread the terms. You have plenty of time to read each question thoroughly and make sure you understand what is being asked. Yet a happy medium must be attained, so don't waste too much time. You must read carefully and efficiently.

☑ Contextual Clues

Look for contextual clues. If the question includes a word you are not familiar with, look at the immediate context for some indication of what the word might mean. Contextual clues can often give you all the information you need to decipher the meaning of an unfamiliar word. Even if you can't determine the meaning, you may be able to narrow down the possibilities enough to make a solid guess at the answer to the question.

☑ Prefixes

If you're having trouble with a word in the question or answer choices, try dissecting it. Take advantage of every clue that the word might include. Prefixes can be a huge help. Usually, they allow you to determine a basic meaning. *Pre-* means before, *post-* means after, *pro-* is positive, *de-* is negative. From prefixes, you can get an idea of the general meaning of the word and try to put it into context.

☑ Hedge Words

Watch out for critical hedge words, such as *likely, may, can, often, almost, mostly, usually, generally, rarely*, and *sometimes*. Question writers insert these hedge phrases to cover every possibility. Often an answer choice will be wrong simply because it leaves no room for exception. Be on guard for answer choices that have definitive words such as *exactly* and *always*.

☑ Switchback Words

Stay alert for *switchbacks*. These are the words and phrases frequently used to alert you to shifts in thought. The most common switchback words are *but, although*, and *however*. Others include *nevertheless, on the other hand, even though, while, in spite of, despite*, and *regardless of*. Switchback words are important to catch because they can change the direction of the question or an answer choice.

⊘ Face Value

When in doubt, use common sense. Accept the situation in the problem at face value. Don't read too much into it. These problems will not require you to make wild assumptions. If you have to go beyond creativity and warp time or space in order to have an answer choice fit the question, then you should move on and consider the other answer choices. These are normal problems rooted in reality. The applicable relationship or explanation may not be readily apparent, but it is there for you to figure out. Use your common sense to interpret anything that isn't clear.

Answer Choice Strategies

⊘ Answer Selection

The most thorough way to pick an answer choice is to identify and eliminate wrong answers until only one is left, then confirm it is the correct answer. Sometimes an answer choice may immediately seem right, but be careful. The test writers will usually put more than one reasonable answer choice on each question, so take a second to read all of them and make sure that the other choices are not equally obvious. As long as you have time left, it is better to read every answer choice than to pick the first one that looks right without checking the others.

⊘ Answer Choice Families

An answer choice family consists of two (in rare cases, three) answer choices that are very similar in construction and cannot all be true at the same time. If you see two answer choices that are direct opposites or parallels, one of them is usually the correct answer. For instance, if one answer choice says that quantity *x* increases and another either says that quantity *x* decreases (opposite) or says that quantity *y* increases (parallel), then those answer choices would fall into the same family. An answer choice that doesn't match the construction of the answer choice family is more likely to be incorrect. Most questions will not have answer choice families, but when they do appear, you should be prepared to recognize them.

⊘ Eliminate Answers

Eliminate answer choices as soon as you realize they are wrong, but make sure you consider all possibilities. If you are eliminating answer choices and realize that the last one you are left with is also wrong, don't panic. Start over and consider each choice again. There may be something you missed the first time that you will realize on the second pass.

⊘ Avoid Fact Traps

Don't be distracted by an answer choice that is factually true but doesn't answer the question. You are looking for the choice that answers the question. Stay focused on what the question is asking for so you don't accidentally pick an answer that is true but incorrect. Always go back to the question and make sure the answer choice you've selected actually answers the question and is not merely a true statement.

⊘ Extreme Statements

In general, you should avoid answers that put forth extreme actions as standard practice or proclaim controversial ideas as established fact. An answer choice that states the "process should be used in certain situations, if..." is much more likely to be correct than one that states the "process should be discontinued completely." The first is a calm rational statement and doesn't even make a definitive, uncompromising stance, using a hedge word *if* to provide wiggle room, whereas the second choice is far more extreme.

☑ BENCHMARK

As you read through the answer choices and you come across one that seems to answer the question well, mentally select that answer choice. This is not your final answer, but it's the one that will help you evaluate the other answer choices. The one that you selected is your benchmark or standard for judging each of the other answer choices. Every other answer choice must be compared to your benchmark. That choice is correct until proven otherwise by another answer choice beating it. If you find a better answer, then that one becomes your new benchmark. Once you've decided that no other choice answers the question as well as your benchmark, you have your final answer.

☑ PREDICT THE ANSWER

Before you even start looking at the answer choices, it is often best to try to predict the answer. When you come up with the answer on your own, it is easier to avoid distractions and traps because you will know exactly what to look for. The right answer choice is unlikely to be word-for-word what you came up with, but it should be a close match. Even if you are confident that you have the right answer, you should still take the time to read each option before moving on.

General Strategies

☑ TOUGH QUESTIONS

If you are stumped on a problem or it appears too hard or too difficult, don't waste time. Move on! Remember though, if you can quickly check for obviously incorrect answer choices, your chances of guessing correctly are greatly improved. Before you completely give up, at least try to knock out a couple of possible answers. Eliminate what you can and then guess at the remaining answer choices before moving on.

☑ CHECK YOUR WORK

Since you will probably not know every term listed and the answer to every question, it is important that you get credit for the ones that you do know. Don't miss any questions through careless mistakes. If at all possible, try to take a second to look back over your answer selection and make sure you've selected the correct answer choice and haven't made a costly careless mistake (such as marking an answer choice that you didn't mean to mark). This quick double check should more than pay for itself in caught mistakes for the time it costs.

☑ PACE YOURSELF

It's easy to be overwhelmed when you're looking at a page full of questions; your mind is confused and full of random thoughts, and the clock is ticking down faster than you would like. Calm down and maintain the pace that you have set for yourself. Especially as you get down to the last few minutes of the test, don't let the small numbers on the clock make you panic. As long as you are on track by monitoring your pace, you are guaranteed to have time for each question.

☑ DON'T RUSH

It is very easy to make errors when you are in a hurry. Maintaining a fast pace in answering questions is pointless if it makes you miss questions that you would have gotten right otherwise. Test writers like to include distracting information and wrong answers that seem right. Taking a little extra time to avoid careless mistakes can make all the difference in your test score. Find a pace that allows you to be confident in the answers that you select.

⊘ Keep Moving

Panicking will not help you pass the test, so do your best to stay calm and keep moving. Taking deep breaths and going through the answer elimination steps you practiced can help to break through a stress barrier and keep your pace.

Final Notes

The combination of a solid foundation of content knowledge and the confidence that comes from practicing your plan for applying that knowledge is the key to maximizing your performance on test day. As your foundation of content knowledge is built up and strengthened, you'll find that the strategies included in this chapter become more and more effective in helping you quickly sift through the distractions and traps of the test to isolate the correct answer.

Now that you're preparing to move forward into the test content chapters of this book, be sure to keep your goal in mind. As you read, think about how you will be able to apply this information on the test. If you've already seen sample questions for the test and you have an idea of the question format and style, try to come up with questions of your own that you can answer based on what you're reading. This will give you valuable practice applying your knowledge in the same ways you can expect to on test day.

Good luck and good studying!

Planning Material Requirements to Support the Master Schedule

Inventory

Inventory is the store of materials a company uses to provide goods and services; these materials include input to production processes like raw materials and materials in process, supplies for maintenance, repair and operation of production processes, and spare parts and finished goods for customers; the ten different types of inventory are raw materials, component parts, work in process, semi-finished goods, finished goods, consigned stock, maintenance, repair and operating supplies, excess inventory, obsolete inventory, and nonconforming inventory.

Inventory management is the process of planning, directing, handling and controlling the inventory so that all necessary items are available when they are required for manufacturing products; inventory management includes placing appropriate orders for materials to meet production needs in a timely fashion as well as storing and valuing items; inventory management is also known as materials scheduling and planning.

Inventory carrying costs are costs incurred by storing materials. These carrying costs include capital costs (the interest paid if the money is borrowed to buy stock, and the opportunity cost of other things the money could have been spent on); costs to insure the stock; monetary loss due to pilferage, spoilage, obsolescence, and deterioration of the stock; and storage and handling costs for the stock. The ordering/set-up costs are the costs incurred placing and processing an order, including the total cost of ordering, receiving, inspecting, and paying for incoming goods, as well as setting up manufacturing.

Ordering/set-up costs are also called preparation costs. Decreasing order size tends to decrease inventory-carrying costs, while increasing order size tends to decrease ordering/set-up costs. Calculating the EOQ minimizes the combined cost of carrying inventory and ordering/setting up.

Terminology regarding inventory:

- Finished goods: Completed products; finished goods are products which have been manufactured, tested, and packaged, and are available for sale to customers as products or associated repair parts; finished goods are also known as end items.
- Finished goods inventory: The store of finished goods kept on hand; products can be manufactured in convenient and economical batches, with extras deposited into finished goods inventory; finished goods inventory provides margin between manufacturing and the customer and decreases the product lead time; finished goods inventory is made up of fluctuation inventory and anticipation inventory.
- Fluctuation inventory: The portion of finished goods inventory that usually remains unused in order to fill unexpected demand for products; fluctuation inventory is also known as safety stock.
- Anticipation inventory: The portion of finished goods inventory that meets the anticipated customer demand for products.
- Excess inventory: Quantities of production materials that are above and beyond what is necessary for safety stock and meeting production demand; unexpected demand fluctuation, engineering changes, and customer order changes can all lead to excess inventory.

- Obsolete inventory: Materials that are unnecessary for production; obsolete inventory differs from excess inventory because excess inventory is the surplus of necessary production materials while obsolete inventory consists of materials that are no longer necessary at all; obsolescence is typically cause by age, new technology or other changes in processes or supplies; obsolete inventory is written off as a loss unless a new use or buyer can be found for the material.
- Nonconforming inventory: Any items, supplied internally or externally, from raw materials to finished goods, which do not meet the requirements or specifications; in the case of nonconforming inventory from suppliers, suppliers are contacted and appropriate action taken, such as destroying the material, returning all or a sample to the supplier, reworking it at the supplier's expense, or sending it to another customer with different standards; in case of internally supplied nonconforming inventory, the quality department and/or material review board (MRB) determine(s) the action to be taken, such as reworking or destroying the material, and preventing future reoccurrences

Raw Materials

Raw materials are the basic purchased or processed materials that serve as input to manufacturing processes and are made into products or product components through those manufacturing processes. Inventory management of raw materials can be handled in different ways depending on the type of business. In custom or make-to-order businesses, raw materials can be ordered as needed to fulfill specific product orders or projects, or materials can be continually replenished so that they are always available for manufacturing. In businesses where predefined products are sold raw materials can be ordered so that they are available in the quantity and at the time necessary to fulfill production requirements within a material requirements planning (MRP) system.

Component parts are raw materials, constituent parts, and other elements that become part of the finished product; raw materials are component parts, but component parts are not necessarily raw materials because raw materials are limited to items that will be used in manufacturing, but component parts are not; the demand for component parts is dependent, and can thus be calculated based on material requirements planning (MRP) production requirements.

Semi-finished goods are incomplete products from all levels of manufacturing held in storage awaiting completion; semi-finished goods differ from work in process (WIP) because semi-finished goods are held in storage while WIP is on the manufacturing floor, but semi-finished goods are often accounted as WIP.

WIP

Work in process (WIP) is materials and incomplete products in various stages of manufacturing. WIP ranges from the raw materials that have entered the flow of processing to the finished goods that have not yet been accepted and added to the finished goods store. In many systems, component parts and semi-finished goods are both considered to be WIP. WIP carries the value accrued up to that point in processing, including costs for material, labor, and overhead, as determined by the company's costing method. The amount of WIP a company maintains is related to the lead time on their materials (longer lead times necessitate more WIP) and the type of business (make-to-order companies may maintain a lot of WIP so that it's available to be finished according to specific orders).

Consigned Stock

Consigned stock, or consignment stock, is goods, usually finished goods, which are owned by the manufacturer but stored at the customer or middleman's site until the customer uses them or the middleman sells them, after which the customer or middleman is charged for them. Consigned stock is usually accounted for and charged per designated time period, typically monthly. This practice is advantageous for the manufacturer because the customer's business is assured and delivery is streamlined, but these advantages are weighed against the holding and opportunity costs of dedicating inventory to one customer. Consigned stock is advantageous to the customers because they have the materials they need continually available for use without investing in inventory. Consigned stock is often used when the customer is a long distance from the supplier in order to streamline delivery and eliminate what would be a long lead time.

SUPPLIES

Terminology regarding operating, maintenance and service supplies;

- Maintenance, repair, and operating supplies (MRO): Supplies used for operation, maintenance, repair and service of the overall production process, and subdivided into maintenance supplies, service supplies, and operating supplies
- Maintenance supplies: Items needed for maintaining and repairing manufacturing equipment; maintenance supplies are also known as spare parts for the equipment; the maintenance engineering department usually handles ordering and storing maintenance supplies; maintenance is scheduled, and associated parts can be ordered and stored according to scheduled maintenance requirements; repair is unexpected, and associated parts can be ordered as needed or kept in inventory using a simple replenishment system
- Service supplies: Items used to replace original parts on the product being manufactured; service supplies are spare parts for the product used in manufacturing and by customers; internal manufacturing demand for service supplies is dependent and can be calculated using material requirements planning (MRP) logic based on the master production schedule; external customer demand for service supplies must be forecasted
- Operating supplies: Items needed for the manufacturing process that do not become part of the product; operating supplies are also known as factory consumables; the value of operating supplies are not usually charged to the product individually, but are counted as factory overhead and are later charged to products through a costing system, although they are increasingly being added to product bills of material to ensure availability and accurate costing

ORDER REVIEW METHODOLOGY

Order review methodology refers to the technique a company uses to make decisions about ordering materials. Decisions to be made include what to order, when to order, how much to order, and when to schedule delivery. Order review methods can be computerized or manual, and the type utilized depends on the type of inventory and the inventory strategy a company uses. Types of order review methods include material requirements planning (MRP), the order point system, the periodic review system, hybrid systems, time phased order point system, and visual review systems.

THE MATERIAL REQUIREMENTS PLANNING (MRP) METHOD OF ORDER REVIEW

The MRP method of order review is based on prioritization. The type and amount of materials to be ordered, the time the order is placed, and the time of delivery are all determined by the master production schedule (MPS). The supplies that will be necessary to meet the future production demands are prioritized and ordered accordingly. The overall purpose of the material requirements planning (MRP) system is to use the master production schedule (MPS), the bills of material, the current inventory records, open purchase orders and other data to determine material schedules and priorities for both purchased and manufactured materials so that everything will be available when necessary to meet the MPS requirements.

MRP logic begins at the end, with the forecast demand and target date for the finished product, and works backward through each required item toward the beginning, the raw materials, with the view of meeting the master production schedule (MPS). If there is not enough of an item to meet the demand on time, then orders are checked to see if there will be enough. If enough have been ordered then the arrival date is checked. If the order will not arrive on time then the order is rescheduled if possible. If the item has not been ordered, then an order is placed. MRP logic applies to purchased items as well as parts manufactured within the company. This sequence is repeated for all materials used in production, from end to beginning. Independent product and material demands are forecasted in the MPS, and dependent material demands are derived from the forecasts.

Order Point System

Orders for additional inventory are made when the number of items available for use has decreased to a predetermined order point (ROP). The number of items available for use is the number in inventory combined with the number on order. ROP is calculated based on the predicted demand per time period (D), the lead time (LT), and the safety stock (SS) using the following formula: ROP=(D*LT)+SS. The number of items to be ordered or economic order quantity (EOQ) is also predetermined. The order point system makes the two following assumptions: demand for the inventory item is constant and independent, and stock should be replenished when used. The order point system is also called the variable cycle, fixed order quantity system because the time between orders varies, but the quantity of the order is always the same.

The Periodic Review System

Item availability is reviewed at regular time intervals. When the review occurs, an order is placed to keep the available items (the number in stock plus on order) at a predetermined target inventory level (TIL). This is in contrast to the order point system, when orders for the same number of parts are placed at irregular time intervals. TIL is determined by summing the anticipated demand during lead time, the anticipated demand during the review cycle, and the safety stock. The number ordered is basically the demand since the previous review, which is the number necessary to restore the TIL. Like the order point system, the periodic review system assumes that demand is constant and independent and that items that have been used should be replenished. The periodic review system is also called the fixed cycle, variable order quantity system because orders always occur at the same frequency, but the quantity of the order varies.

Hybrid Systems

Combinations of order point and periodic review systems that were developed to offset the limitations of both; the two common hybrids are the periodic/order point system and the optional replenishment system

- Periodic/order point system: A hybrid system combining the periodic review system and the order point system that protects against shortages due to the constant demand assumption of the periodic review system not being met; the periodic/order point system is basically the periodic review system with a re-order point in place as a safety check to prevent running out of inventory when demand is not constant but increases unexpectedly; inventory is checked at regular time intervals and restocked accordingly, but there is also a reorder point in place so that materials would be re-stocked before the regular time if necessary

- Optional replenishment system: A hybrid of the periodic review and order point systems with an additional common sense check. Material availability is reviewed at fixed time intervals, but materials can be ordered before the fixed time interval if the available stock decreases to the order point (ROP). Conversely, an order does not have to be placed at the fixed review time if the available stock has not decreased to the common sense maximum availability at which orders can be placed. Order quantities are set to maintain the predetermined target inventory level (TIL). This system protects against unrealistically small orders when the demand is unexpectedly low and shortages when the demand is unexpectedly high, both of which can occur when the replenishment and constant demand assumptions of the periodic review and order point systems do not hold true.

Time Phased Order Point System

In the order point system, a single order is placed when the number of available items decreases to the predetermined re-order point (ROP). When the system is time-phased, projected future demand is also taken into account, like in the MRP system, and the demand does not have to be constant like it does for the order point system. There is a calculated ROP, at which time an order can be made to replenish inventory after use, and there is also an MRP-type order schedule to prepare for future demand. Both past use and future demand are accounted for in deciding when to order, so changes in demand do not pose a problem to the system like they do in the order point system.

Visual Review System

The process of visually checking inventory to gauge reordering needs; one example of a visual review system is keeping the inventory item in a bin that is marked in some way with the re-order point (ROP), and reordering when the bin level decreases to the ROP marking

Two-Bin System

An organized visual review system in which there are two bins holding the inventory item; one bin is open for use, while the other bin is sealed; the sealed bin holds the average demand during lead time plus the safety stock; when the open bin runs out, it is refilled with the contents of the sealed bin, at which time an order is placed; the contents of the reserve sealed bin should last until the new order arrives, at which point the sealed reserve bin is reestablished

Lot Sizes

Determining Lot Size

Lot-sizing techniques are methods used to determine the quantity of items to order; the two main types of lot-sizing techniques are demand rate techniques and discrete lot-sizing techniques

- Demand rate techniques: Methods used to determine the number of items to order based on product demand; demand rate techniques include the fixed order quantity and the economic order quantity (EOC) techniques.
- The fixed order quantity lot-sizing technique: A demand rate technique also called the variable time, fixed quantity method. In the fixed order quantity technique, orders are always placed for the same predetermined amount of items, but the length of time between orders varies. The fixed amount to order can be determined in several ways. One way is based on supplier restrictions. Order quantity is fixed to the amount the supplier can produce or deliver at one time. The amount to order can also be fixed by the supplier's or the company's own storage restrictions. Another method for setting the fixed order amount is the economic order quantity (EOQ). Regardless of how the fixed order quantity is set, if it is not high enough to meet current demand, a second order for the same amount is placed.

- The EOQ technique: A demand rate, fixed order quantity technique for determining order lot size. In this technique, the EOQ is calculated to determine the most economical lot size. The two main costs associated with order quantity and upon which the EOQ is based are inventory carrying costs and ordering/set-up costs. The EOQ is the order quantity at which total cost (inventory carrying and ordering/setting up costs combined) is minimized. The EOQ is calculated according to the formula EOQ=Sqrt (2US/IC), where EOQ is the economic order quantity (the fixed lot size), U is the annual quantity ordered, S is the ordering or set-up cost, I is the inventory holding cost, and C is the cost per individual item.
- Discrete lot-sizing techniques: Methods of determining the number of items to order based on the MRP-calculated requirements for given periods; the amount required is the amount ordered and no surplus remains for later periods; both the lot for lot method and the period order quantity (POQ) method are discrete lot-sizing techniques.
- Lot for lot technique: A discrete lot-sizing method in which orders are made for the exact number of materials necessary to meet production requirements for one period; it is important to remember and account for the fact that ordering system time periods are usually one day.
- Period order quantity technique (POQ): A discrete lot-sizing method in which orders are made for the exact number of materials necessary to meet production requirements for a variable given number of time periods; the given number of periods does not begin until a period with demand for ordered materials, but periods with no demand once the set of periods has started are not ignored; the number of periods is chosen to optimize ordering and holding costs

Batching Rules

Lot-sizing techniques produce a theoretical number of items to be ordered, but these theoretical lot sizes are not necessarily feasible. Batching rules bring theory into practice. Examples of batching rules are minimum order quantity, maximum order quantity, and multiple order quantity. The minimum order quantity rule sets the smallest number of parts that can be ordered. This minimum is usually required by the supplier to cover set-up costs incurred in filling the order. The maximum order quantity rule sets the largest number that can be ordered at one time. Maximum order quantity can be set for reasons such as space and weight restrictions and long processing times. Multiple order quantity is related to item grouping. When items are not sold individually but in sets, orders must be made in sets by rounding the calculated lot size up to the nearest set multiple.

Safety Stock and Lead Time

Safety stock is the material kept in inventory at all times to protect against variability in demand, stock replenishment time, and supplier service level; three techniques for determining safety stock are statistical, time period, and fixed

Safety lead time is a time buffer added to the actual or calculated lead time to protect against lead time fluctuations and insure that required material is available when it is necessary; safety lead time is used when the supplier is habitually late or inconsistent with order timing; it is also useful in place of safety stock when items are ordered as needed and not stocked; safety lead time can also be called safety time

Statistical safety stock is a method for calculating the quantity of safety stock to keep on hand at all times in order to protect specifically against statistical fluctuations in supply of materials and demand for products. The formula for statistical safety stock is SS=S*SF*[Sqrt(L/FP)] or SS=1.25*MAD*SF*[Sqrt(L/FP)], where SS is the safety stock, S is the standard deviation, SF is the safety factor, L is the lead time, FP is the forecast time period, and MAD is the mean absolute deviation. Associated formulas are S=(1.25*MAD) and MAD=(ABSUM/N), where ABSUM is the cumulative sum of absolute deviations between forecast and actual demand in time periods considered and N is the number of time periods. The safety factor (SF) is the number of standard deviations (Ss) or mean average deviations (MADs) used to provide the desired finished goods service level. SF is looked up according to desired service level on the table of safety factors for normal distribution.

Time Period Safety Stock

Time period safety stock is a simple calculation based on the quantity of parts necessary to meet demand during a predetermined time period. Time period safety stock is recalculated for each time period based on that time period's demand, so the time period safety stock quantity changes as the demand changes. The formula for time period safety stock is SS=F*T, where SS is the safety stock, F is the forecast usage for the time period, and T is the length of the time period for which the safety stock is valid. The time period technique for determining safety stock is used when the supply reliability is uncertain.

Fixed Safety Stock

A predetermined quantity of safety stock set without respect to demand, demand variation, usage, or supplier dependability. Fixed safety stock quantities can be used for new products, products being phased out, and in other special cases. With new products there is no history available for calculating a safety stock, so a fixed quantity is set to protect against running out until there is history with which to work to determine a more appropriate safety stock. Products being phased out do not require a safety stock at all, so the fixed quantity is zero.

Tracking Signals

Tracking signals are used to monitor the accuracy of the forecast demand in relation to the actual demand, and signal when the forecast demand may be inappropriate and must be reviewed. The tracking signal is calculated as follows: TS=(SUM/MAD), where MAD=(ABSUM/N); TS is the tracking signal, SUM is the algebraic sum of deviations between forecast and actual demand during the time periods considered, MAD is the mean average deviation, ABSUM is the sum of absolute deviations between forecast and actual demand during the time periods considered, and N is the number of time periods considered. The forecast demand must be revisited when the tracking signal reaches positive or negative four. Tracking signals are useful when there are a large number of items to forecast manually, since the minor items could be easily overlooked. The tracking signal indicates when the forecast and actual demands of minor items have become incompatible and attention is required.

Inventory Value and Accounting

Inventory valuation and accounting terms:

- Inventory valuation: The process of assigning monetary value to stock held in inventory; the value of inventory includes purchase cost of raw materials and other parts, as well as value added through processing
- Perpetual inventory accounting: The process of continually maintaining a record of all inventory; every individual receipt and release of inventory stock is recorded; in perpetual inventory accounting inventory records should always be up to date

- Periodic inventory accounting: The process of keeping inventory records by occasionally counting all inventory on hand; inventory receipts and releases are not individually recorded and records are only as up-to-date as the last count; periodic inventory accounting is not feasible in situations where exact, current inventory levels are regularly required, such as when material requirements planning (MRP) is practiced

LIFO

In the LIFO method of inventory valuation the most recently received inventory items are used first, hence the name last in first out. The financial value assigned to the items is the individual price that was actually paid for them. The older parts, which may have been cheaper, remain in storage. Since the most recently purchased items valued at their purchase price are used first, inventory values of materials being used in production and thus production costs also more quickly reflect changes in material prices, rather than deflecting the effects of changes to later production. When prices increase, the cost to the producer of the goods sold goes up more quickly, causing profits to decrease more quickly. In the LIFO method, the internal cost to the producer of the goods sold better reflects the current market situation.

FIFO (First in first out)

An inventory valuation method in which the items are used in the same order in which they are received from the supplier; like in the LIFO method, the materials are valued at the price actually paid for them (actual individual cost per item); when material prices increase, since the materials are used in the order they were received and valued at the price actually paid for them, the inventory values of stock being used do not reflect the price increase until the older, cheaper stock is used up; FIFO delays the effect of inflation, maximizing profits in the meantime through minimizing the cost to the producer of goods sold; the internal cost of goods sold less accurately reflects the current market situation than the LIFO method

Transfer costing

A method of inventory valuation used to value inventory that has been transferred within the company without being sold; the economic value assigned to the transferred material is usually the actual or standard cost, and transportation costs for the transfer may be added to the value

Standard costing

Standard costing is based on the target or theoretical cost of materials, labor, and overhead. The standard cost is calculated by determining the current actual cost at the beginning of a predetermined time period (usually a year or a quarter), estimating what the actual cost will be at the end of the time period accounting for inflation and other price changes, and averaging the time period starting cost and estimated ending cost. This average is the standard cost. When the standard cost is recalculated, current inventory is revalued to the new standard cost. The standard cost must be checked against actual cost, so that differences can be accounted for within the system through a variance account and forecasting can be adjusted if necessary to minimize differences in the future. Assigning inventory values through standard costing stabilizes prices, which in turn simplifies manufacturing management and determination of sale prices.

Weighted moving average

Value is assigned to inventory based on the average value of the stock held at that time. Inflation, deflation, and other price changes are spread out through all of the current stock, so the effect of price change is felt more slowly. The weighted moving average is calculated by adding the cost of the new items to the total value of the items already in stock, and then dividing by the total number of items (old and new). The weighted moving average is recalculated with each new batch of inventory, and all current stock of the item (old and new) is revalued accordingly. When using the weighted moving average, it is not necessary to value inventory items or batches individually, because all like items in stock have the same value.

PROCESS COSTING

A method of inventory valuation in which value added to the inventory by the production process is set based on average cost per unit; instead of tracking actual production costs per item, the total cost of production for a particular time period or lot is tracked, and then divided equally among all of the materials processed during that time or in that lot; this average process cost is added to the inventory value of each item; the work done on one item in the process is called an equivalent unit of production; process costing is used in high volume production settings

EQUIVALENT UNIT OF PRODUCTION

A concept that is used in process costing; the complete processing done on one item, to which an economic cost is assigned by averaging (summing the total cost of the process and dividing by the number of items processed); work in process is typically assumed to be half-finished, or 50% of an equivalent unit

PROJECT COSTING

A method of inventory valuation in which actual costs are tracked for an overall project, and not for individual products or processes; this method is used in industries oriented toward customer service, where projects are highly specific, not repeated, and geared toward individual customers; the project cost is all actual or standard costs incurred while executing the project

ACTUAL COSTING

A method of inventory valuation based on the actual costs of material, labor, and overhead used to produce an item; costs are tracked and recorded as they occur in manufacturing, and attributed appropriately to the individual items produced

INVENTORY ACCURACY

Inventory accuracy is the extent to which inventory records actually reflect the physical store of materials. Inventory accuracy is a key element in providing materials for manufacturing on a timely basis and in achieving customer satisfaction. Inventory records are kept for material orders, raw materials, work in process, shortages, and finished goods. Inaccurate inventory records cause many problems in manufacturing. Having fewer materials than the records indicate can cause material shortages, which lead to delays in manufacturing, increased shipping costs due to expediting orders (both materials in and products out), late deliveries of products to customers, and lost sales. Having more materials than the records indicate can cause material excesses, which lead to higher obsolescence and storage costs. Methods for insuring inventory accuracy include annual inventory, cycle counting, control groups, and standard containers.

Two primary factors that impact inventory accuracy are tools and personnel. The tools necessary to maintain a high level of accuracy include appropriate counting equipment, sufficient space for storage of materials including sub-stores if necessary, containers to hold the materials, an effective item identification and location system, and isolated storage for nonconforming materials. Personnel must be properly trained in how to execute the job; they must clearly bear responsibility for inventory accuracy in their job requirements; they must wield the authority necessary to maintain inventory accuracy through use of tools such as locked stores and documentation control; and they must be held accountable for the resulting accuracy level.

Terms regarding inventory accuracy:

- Auditor: The person whose job includes reconciling a company's theoretical and actual assets; within a manufacturing environment auditing includes reconciling actual inventory with inventory records; inventory auditing is carried out in two different ways, annual inventory and cycle counting
- Annual inventory: The process of physically counting all of the materials in storage one time per year, comparing the results with the inventory records, and resolving any differences in order to maintain inventory accuracy.
- Cycle counting: The ongoing process of physically counting storage materials according to a predetermined schedule and resolving differences between the physical store and the records in order to maintain inventory accuracy; usually the more used or higher value items are counted more often, while less used or lower value items are counted less often (ABC schedule); cycle counting is performed by dedicated personnel; in addition to maintaining inventory accuracy, cycle counting helps uncover and alleviate inventory errors and provides a higher level of accuracy than annual inventory.
- Control group: The process of physically counting a predetermined set of inventory items at regular, frequent intervals in order to uncover and alleviate inventory errors quickly in situations where inventory accuracy is low; improvements can then be made to the overall inventory accuracy based on findings; control group is a method for quickly improving .inventory accuracy, rather than a method for maintaining accuracy.
- Standard containers: Bins, cartons, or boxes, of the same size and usually reusable, which are used to hold parts during transportation and storage; inventory counting is simplified and accuracy is increased because each container holds the same amount of material

Methods of Verifying Count Accuracy During Annual Inventory

Methods for verifying count accuracy during annual inventory include sampling, double counting, and verifying. In sampling, a few of the inventory items are counted a second time to insure overall accuracy. In double counting, all materials are counted two times by different individuals or teams to insure accuracy. In verifying, there is someone with the counter or counting team verifying and recording their results to insure accuracy. Verifying accuracy of annual inventory may be necessary because those involved are often not dedicated inventory workers, so they may lack skill or not take the process seriously.

Customer Service

Customer service is a company's ability to relate to their customers to transact sales, aid in customer use of products, and meet any other needs the customer might have, all according to the customer's specified quality, quantity and time table; customer service is usually carried out by a dedicated department that acts as a liaison between manufacturing and the customer; service level, stock out percentage, safety factors, backlog, responsiveness, quality, and cost of service are all customer service issues

Service level is a quantitative measure of customer service; the percentage of orders, order line items, or order dollar amounts that the company fills successfully according to the customer's required quality, quantity, and time table; in industries with ready-made products, the percentage may be calculated based on items in stock when the order is received, a possibly stricter criteria than meeting the customer's deadlines

Performance

A company's performance, as judged by their customers, is based on three characteristics. These characteristics, in order of importance, are product quality, timeliness of delivery, and price. Quality is the most important because it is essential. Items that do not meet the customer's quality requirements are not fit for the customer to use. Timely arrival and low price are worthless without an acceptable quality level. Once it is established that a company provides usable products, the next consideration is timeliness. After receiving goods that are fit for use, customers prioritize receiving goods in sufficient time to meet schedule requirements. Price considerations are subordinate to both quality and time considerations. Savings on the cost of goods are not worth the costs of poor quality and late delivery.

Accuracy Target and Tolerance

Inventory accuracy target is a company's goal for the level of accuracy between the inventory records and the actual balances of inventory stocks; the inventory accuracy is calculated as the percentage of stock items whose inventory counts on record fall within the tolerance level of the actual number in stock; for use of computerized inventory management systems, inventory accuracy targets must be 100% in order to achieve the minimum 95% accuracy necessary for the system to be feasible, otherwise there would be an unreasonable number of inventory excesses and shortages.

Tolerance is the amount of discrepancy allowable between the inventory record and the actual balance of inventory stock; allowance for acceptable error, attributable primarily to counting equipment error.

Demand Issues

Types of demand:

- Independent demand: Demand for material, usually finished goods, which cannot be calculated internally and is unrelated to internal factors, but which must be predicted; for example, a company's estimation or projection of the amount of finished goods that will be necessary to meet customer orders in a given future time period is an independent demand on manufacturing
- Dependent demand: Demand for materials, usually raw materials or component parts, which is not predicted or forecast, but rather can be calculated from the independent demand; for example, once the independent demand for finished goods is forecast, the number of component parts and raw materials necessary to manufacture the forecast number of finished goods can be calculated
- Assembly demand: Demand for finished goods which is predicted based on past average demand and other factors; an independent demand for products
- Component demand: Demand for component parts which is dependent on and calculated from the assembly or finished goods demand; usually lumpy since it is dictated by the assembly stock ordering method (at reorder points, there is high component demand, but between order points there is no demand)

Lumpy Demand

Lumpy demand is irregular, discontinuous, uneven demand, which is characterized by periods of high and steady demand alternating with periods of no demand. Lumpy component demand is created by finished goods or assembly batching, when all components necessary for the entire batch are demanded at one time followed by a period of no demand which lasts until the next manufacturing batch requires the associated component parts. Lumpy assembly or finished goods demand is created by customers who vary greatly in their ordering habits or end items that are seasonal in nature.

Performance Measurement

Inventory performance is the effectiveness and efficiency with which a company acquires and uses inventory in order to meet productions goals and demand for products.

Inventory performance measurements are specific calculations used to quantitatively measure inventory performance; inventory performance measurements help a company establish norms, set guidelines, identify problems and improve performance; inventory performance measurements include inventory turnover, customer service level, and inventory accuracy.

Inventory turnover is a measurement of inventory investment and usage, based on the number of times a company goes through its inventory in a set time period, typically one year; inventory turnover is calculated as the ratio of the cost of goods sold for the period (usually yearly) to the actual or standard cost of the average inventory in stock (usually determined quarterly); inventory turnover can be calculated based on actual historical figures or future forecasted figures; higher values are usually considered more efficient, but values vary greatly between industries and companies; inventory turnover can also be called stock turns.

Necessary information for inventory planning for the materials or inventory planning process are inventory data, master schedule data, and engineering data. Having complete, accurate, and up-to-date data is essential to the inventory planning process. Bills of material, purchase order records, work in process balances, and physical inventory balances must all be maintained accurately, completely, and as changes occur so that neither material shortages nor material excesses result from material resource planning (MRP) decisions based on faulty information. Work in process data is especially challenging to maintain because of the production environment.

Inventory data is specific information about the individual items kept in stock for production as well as the policies and techniques related to those items, including description, size, fabrication, usage, demand history, current balance, storage location, classification, ordering method, safety stock, and safety lead time; the two primary records of inventory data are the item master data file and the inventory stock status report.

Item master data file is a record of all of the information about a particular part, including physical, ordering, costing, design, fabrication, and planning information along with associated policies and techniques; both static information and dynamic information are included; specific examples of data kept in the item master file are the part description, storage location(s), primary and secondary units of measure along with conversion factors, manufacturing lead time, balance on hand, quantity allocated, quantity on order, order quantity, safety stock, safety lead time, ordering methods, and ABC classification.

Stock

Terms regarding stock issues:

- Assembly stock: The finished goods kept in stock in order to fill customer orders; the order point or time-phased order point methods are used to signal manufacturing to produce more finished goods stock; assembly safety stock is maintained to protect against demand variations and delays in manufacturing.

- Component stock: The store of components maintained to fill component demand. Component stock holds constant at the order quantity plus safety stock until components are released into production to fulfill component demand, at which point component stock falls to the safety stock. If component stock is replenished as it is used according to the order point method, stock is held for longer periods of time before use; if component stock is replenished as it is needed according to the time-phased order point method, stock is held for shorter periods of time before use. Safety stock is kept to protect against demand variations and late deliveries.
- Inventory stock status report: A record of the most important and frequently used information about a particular part, a summary of the item master data file; item information included in the inventory stock status report can be inventory or stock on hand, open orders, demand history, critical or free stock, projected available balance, projected on-hand balance, quarantined stock, floor stock, safety stock and year-to-date demand.
- Critical stock: In stock and available for use, not including planned stock issues; also known as free stock.
- Projected available balance: The quantity of stock that will be available in the future including current stock, open orders, and planned orders.
- Projected on-hand balance: The quantity of stock that will be available in the future, including only current stock and open orders.
- Quarantined stock: The material isolated from regular inventory because they are suspected of not meeting specifications or requirement.
- Floor stock: Production material available on the manufacturing floor as needed; these inventory releases are not recorded but reconstructed from the number of end items produced.

Scheduling

Scheduling terms:

- Master schedule data: Specific information about the parts, quantities of parts, acquisition of parts through manufacture and/or purchase, and timing and prioritization necessary to make individual item plans in order to meet the MPS created through the master scheduling process.
- Master schedule: A target production calendar set by management based on the forecast demand for products; the master schedule includes supply, inventory, and demand.
- Master production schedule (MPS): A production schedule developed from a portion of the master schedule in which individual items are broken down, quantified, scheduled, and prioritized in order to meet production demands.
- Master schedule horizon: The time period into the future which is covered by the master schedule; the master schedule horizon must be long enough to allow time for ordering materials and manufacturing products; the master schedule horizon is divided by time fences into three parts, the final assembly stage, the manufacturing and purchasing stage, and the look-ahead period.
- Time fences: The endpoints of the three periods of the master schedule horizon, specifically the demand time fence, the planning time fence, and the planning horizon.
- Feasibility of the master production schedule (MPS): The extent to which meeting the MPS is possible given the material and production constraints; MPS time fences and rough cut capacity planning (RCCP) are used to insure MPS feasibility.

Time Periods

From the beginning of the master schedule horizon until the demand time fence is the final assembly period, also known as the frozen period. The length of the final assembly period and thus the date of the demand time fence is set based on the amount of time necessary for final manufacturing. The period is referred to as frozen because changes within this time are costly since processing has already started. The chief executive must usually approve changes during the final assembly time period.

The second stage of the master schedule horizon is the manufacturing and purchasing period, also called the flexible period. This period lasts from the demand time fence until the planning time fence, and is set by the time necessary for procurement of materials and initial manufacturing processes. From the beginning of the master schedule horizon until the end of the flexible period is the total manufacturing lead time. Changes can be made within this window by the master scheduler, based on material and capacity availability.

From the planning time fence until the planning horizon is the look ahead or batching period. This period is the length of time necessary to replenish inventory stores for future production, and is based on the company's batching rules. However far ahead in time a company orders any of its parts is the length of time necessary for the look-ahead period. Changes during this period are relatively easy and handled by the master scheduler based on the production capacity. Materials are not a consideration since there is sufficient time available to acquire whatever is necessary.

Bill of Material

A bill of material (BOM) is a specification of all of the contents used to build a product, an intermediate assembly, or other parent part, including raw materials, component parts, intermediate assemblies, and their quantities and interrelationships. The overall BOM usually includes the actual BOM for item content breakdowns as well as the item master file for information on the individual parts used to build. The BOM includes all product structure records for items used to build the parent part. Alternatively, a BOM can be a specification of all materials and other parts necessary for a contract manufacturer to produce a batch of component parts for a customer. The BOM can also be known as a recipe, formulation, or ingredient list.

Explosions and Implosions

BOMs are typically formatted as BOM explosions or BOM implosions. An explosion focuses on the production of one part. BOM information is displayed in a format that shows the lower level parts used to manufacture a part. A BOM implosion focuses on the part itself and the parent parts it is used to build, rather than the parts of which it is made. Information is displayed for all production uses of the part, showing all the different parent parts the item is used in. In short, a BOM explosion shows us how a particular part is built from other parts, and a BOM implosion shows us all the ways a particular part can be used to make other parts.

Single Level and Multi-Level

The two types of BOMs are single level and multi-level. Single level BOMs contain only the immediately preceding level of the product structure, the last level of components and processing through which the part is manufactured. Other BOMs must be referenced to see the earlier manufacturing steps and components that went into forming the part. In a multi-level BOM, the lower level BOMs are all incorporated, and the multiple processing steps necessary to manufacture a part can be seen at one time, rather than just the immediately preceding step in manufacturing.

MATERIAL REQUIREMENTS PLANNING

Requirements for running an MRP system are a computer, bills of material (BOM), inventory records, and a master production schedule (MPS). A computer or computer system is necessary for storing and linking information as well as performing MRP calculations. Although the calculations are simple, the volume of calculations requires a computer. Bills of material provide input values for the MRP calculations. Inventory records include purchase orders, raw materials, work in process, and finished goods, and establish current inventory standing. The MPS drives the whole MRP system. All MRP calculations depend on the MPS. Furthermore, the MPS must be stable and realistic. All demands within production will change as the MPS changes, so MPS change must be minimized. Also, the MPS must be realistic or MRP is a waste of time since the calculations will not come close to meeting the actual demand. Minimum BOM accuracy of 99% and minimum inventory record accuracy of 95% are necessary for the correct parts to be ordered on a consistent basis.

CHARACTERISTICS

When considering the development or purchase of an MRP system, it is important to consider the system characteristics. The three types of MRP characteristics to be considered are design characteristics, performance characteristics and operational characteristics. Design characteristics involve the fundamentals of the system: the parameters to be set along with the functions and features through which material requirements are scheduled and other decisions are made. Key design characteristics include inputs and outputs, planning horizon, time buckets, re-planning frequency, requirements traceability, and order status. Performance characteristics refer to a system's mechanisms for handling changes: how quickly changes are analyzed and feasible alternative plans are made. Key performance characteristics include directive messages and performance measurements. Operational characteristics relate to usability and personnel and include types, timing and reporting of order actions, system nervousness, and personnel training.

INPUTS AND OUTPUTS

Inputs and outputs are basic pieces of information (inputs) from which MRP software creates data tables and status reports as well as calculates directive messages (outputs); the basic inputs to an MRP system are item master files, master production schedules (MPS), bills of material, lead times, scrap rates, inventory records (95% minimum accuracy), service part demand, and safety stock; MRP system outputs are basic data, status reports, and directive messages; directive messages include actions to be taken and exceptions to the plan which have occurred

PLANNING HORIZON

In an MRP system, the planning horizon is taken directly from the master production schedule (MPS) where it has usually been set at the cumulative lead time plus a look-ahead period

TIME BUCKETS

A time bucket is a set time period for which MRP information is summarized. The information can be used for both calculation and reporting purposes. Time buckets for calculations are often smaller than reporting time buckets since greater accuracy is required. One week is considered the largest feasible time bucket for current and near-future detailed planning, but plans further into the future can have larger time buckets. When using time buckets some accuracy is lost since information is generalized to the whole time bucket. For example, an order must arrive by a certain time bucket rather than by a certain day. Historically, time buckets were used to condense information to decrease computer space and memory demands, but they are no longer necessary since current computer technology is capable of maintaining daily information and scheduling.

Re-planning Frequency

The re-planning frequency is the rate at which MRP calculations and resulting schedules are refigured. Re-planning frequency is closely associated with regeneration runs and net change runs, both of which are re-planning methodologies. In regeneration runs, the MRP system starts again at the beginning with the master production schedule (MPS), which is exploded to include all bills of material in order to re-calculate all material requirements. Net change runs involve exploding and re-calculating only those portions of the plan that have been changed or are affected by a change. These two methods can be used in conjunction, with net change runs performed at a higher frequency and regeneration runs performed at a lower frequency or only when major changes occur.

Requirements Traceability

Requirements traceability is the MRP system's ability to track the source of calculated part requirements. Requirements traceability is necessary in MRP since the same part can be used at more than one stage of the production process. All of the different requirements for one part are added together to form a total requirement which is the number ordered, so the resulting part inventory may have several different uses throughout production. It is through tracing requirements that we know what those different uses are and how to allocate the parts in stock among them. MRP requirements traceability is achieved through a process called pegging.

Pegging

Pegging is the process used to provide requirements traceability within an MRP system. Pegging provides requirements traceability by including the parent part(s) generating the demand for the component in the component requirement record. Pegging can be single-level or multi-level. Single-level pegging includes only the immediate parent part generating the demand in the component requirement record, which can then be traced through the parent part's requirement record and further if necessary. Multi-level pegging includes sources of demand from the immediate parent all the way to the original customer order or demand forecast in the component requirement record.

Order Status

Order status is the standing of an order within the order planning and execution process. Possible order statuses are planned orders, firm planned orders, and scheduled receipts. Planned orders are orders that have been prompted within the MRP system in order to make materials available to meet master production schedule (MPS) requirements, but have not yet been confirmed by the planner or placed, and can be changed automatically as necessary when other changes occur. Firm planned orders are orders which have not been placed but have been confirmed by the planner, so the order date, quantity, and delivery time are set and cannot be changed without the planner's approval. Scheduled receipts are external orders that have already been placed or internal orders for which processing has begun and therefore have a set delivery or completion date.

Directive Messages

The purpose of MRP is to plan and schedule materials to be available to meet production requirements as set forth by the master production schedule (MPS). The MRP system produces prompts for actions necessary to meet these production requirements for materials. These prompts are in the form of directive messages. Examples of tasks prompted by directive messages are confirming orders, placing orders with suppliers, releasing orders to manufacturing, and rescheduling in response to system changes. Directive messages are also called action messages and exception messages. Action messages and exception messages are sometimes differentiated. When differentiated, action messages can be considered business as usual. They are prompts for actions to meet the production schedule. Exception messages deal with problems that arise. They are prompts for actions when the schedule is not being met or there have been system changes.

Performance Measurements

Performance measurements are metrics in place within the MRP system to measure the extent to which material planning goals are being met. Good performance measurements are easily understandable, usable, and clearly related to the goals. MRP performance measurements typically monitor timeliness, completion, number of directive messages generated, and value. Timeliness for confirming orders, releasing orders, completing internal orders, and storing end items in finished goods can all be measured against their target dates. Completion of orders can be measured against target quantities to detect shortages. The number of directive messages, both action and exception messages, produced in a given time period can be counted. Values of the actual material stores and work in process can be calculated and compared to the target values.

Types of Order Actions

An important operational characteristic of an MRP system is the types of action messages generated. MRP systems function to meet master production schedule (MPS) requirements by storing information, performing calculations using the stored information, and creating action messages in response to the calculation results. A simple system may send only the most basic type of action message, a prompt to release a material order. At this point the planner would complete a planned or firm planned order by actually placing the order with an external supplier or releasing the order into manufacturing along with any associated steps. In addition to completing the order, the planner must report within the system that the action is being performed. More complex systems break down the ordering process to multiple steps, generating several action messages and requiring several corresponding responses. Order action messages can be broken down to include steps associated with ordering like producing the paperwork for an internal order, issuing the paperwork to inventory, and releasing the order to manufacturing.

Timing of Order Actions

Order action timing and reporting are important operational characteristics of an MRP system. Order action timing refers to the frequency with which action messages are generated by the system and the corresponding due dates assigned to the actions. Timing is related to the re-planning frequency of the system, how often regeneration runs and net change runs are performed. Weekly re-planning gives the scheduler a weekly series of action messages, which her or she performs and reports before the next weekly update. This is usually more time than necessary for performance of individual items, and too much leeway for responding promptly to changes. Most manufacturing is moving toward a daily re-planning frequency producing corresponding daily action messages. Action due dates, or lead times, are then related to the actual time required for performance of the prompted action and are not unnecessarily long.

Reporting of Order Actions

Reporting order actions is an MRP system's mechanism for order action accountability. When the planner has completed the prompted order actions, a report is made within the MRP system reflecting that. There is much diversity within MRP systems in how order actions are reported. Typically, when the planner has completed a prompted order action, her or she looks up the order on the system and changes its status designation. In other cases, the entry of inventory releases to production or other order-related activity can trigger the change in order status automatically within the MRP system and no separate reporting action is necessary. In some systems, the order action messages themselves have convenient associated screens for the planner to make and report the recommended changes simultaneously. Reporting order actions is an operational characteristic of MRP systems that must be considered when choosing or developing one.

System Nervousness

System nervousness is the level of change in current, low level ordering activity caused by small or distant upper level changes. When a change occurs in the inventory or master production schedule (MPS), all levels below the change are affected and some re-planning and rescheduling must occur; however, the system response to the change can be unreasonable and unnecessary. For example, generating many action messages to be handled immediately because a delivery six months in the future is scheduled one day off is neither efficient nor effective in most cases. A mechanism for decreasing system nervousness is a sensitivity filter. Sensitivity filters stabilize planning by providing a buffer between changes and resulting action messages. Using a sensitivity filter, it is possible to set the system so that target dates and expected actual dates can be within a certain specified tolerance of each other, and not exact, without generating action messages. Sensitivity filters do cloak the real situation, so they must be used with caution and based on the specific circumstances.

Education and Training

Appropriate personnel training at all levels is essential to the successful implementation and maintenance of an MRP system. The need for training is commonly unrecognized, and therefore training is often underestimated and under budgeted. Unfortunately, insufficient training can result in system failure. The first step in training is assessment, or determining who needs training and what training they need. Executives and managers must understand the principles of MRP. The system users must understand not only the general principles of MRP but also the practicalities of how those principles are applied in their particular MRP system and the rules and methods applied to the system within their company. Simulation training and industry- and product-specific training are especially useful. The timeliness of the training is also of paramount importance. Workers must be trained before they must perform, but not so early that they are not yet interested.

Detailed Planning Process

Steps in the Process

The three steps in the detailed material planning process are initializing data, exploding the bills of material, and time phasing material requirements. Initializing data, the first step in detailed material planning, is providing the information from which material planning calculations are made. There are three data types, fixed data, inventory data, and requirements data. The second step in detailed material planning is exploding the bills of material. Through exploding the bills of material, the overall product demand is broken down into individual demand for all of the necessary parts for the production process. The last step in detailed material planning is time phasing the material requirements. Time phasing material requirements involves attaching dates to all of the individual demands for materials, for the near and distant future. Like calculating the demand for individual parts from the product demand, target dates for item availability are set by working backward from the finished product target date or order due date, taking into account the times necessary to perform all manufacturing steps.

Fixed Data, Inventory Data, and Requirements Data

- Fixed data: Part of the initial data for detailed material planning from which calculations can be made; fixed data describes individual materials used in production and, as the name implies, does not change often; fixed data includes item descriptions, safety stock quantities, lot-sizing rules, scrap and yield information, lead times, and bills of material.

- Inventory data: Part of the initial data for detailed material planning from which calculations can be made; inventory data is information regarding current stock and orders to be received; inventory data changes continually and must be kept up-to-date; inventory data includes stock on hand, open orders, and scheduled receipts.
- Requirements data: Part of the initial data in detailed material planning that can be calculated from fixed data, inventory data and master schedule requirements; requirements data is information about the demand for all items used and produced throughout the production process; requirements data includes component requirement records, gross requirements, and material allocations.

Explosion Process

The second step in detailed material planning is exploding the bills of material through all levels of production for a product. Through the explosion process, the overall product demand is broken down into individual demand for all raw materials, component parts, and other parts required for the production process. These individual demands are then compared to inventory records to determine net requirements. This process of using the gross requirements and other fixed data to determine net requirements is referred to as netting. Netting is performed through a material requirements planning (MRP) system, order configurators or other methods along with ordering and safety stock techniques. The net requirements are used as the basis for ordering decisions to provide materials to meet demand.

Level-by-Level Processing and Low Level Codes

In order to provide material to meet demand, an MRP system uses MRP logic to prevent material shortages during production. As netting is performed, net requirements are generated. When a net requirement is generated within an MRP system, an order is planned and a requirement record is created for the part. The process of netting is performed on a level-by-level basis, meaning that, working backwards from a finished product in its product structure, netting for the entire level immediately preceding the finished product is completed before proceeding to the level before that. Level-by-level processing is used along with low level coding to insure that net requirements are complete before orders are generated, since parts can be used at more than one level in the product structure. Netting an entire level before moving to the next level, and not acting on net requirements until the item's low-level code is reached prevent generation of orders based on incomplete net requirements.

Projected Available Balance, Net Requirements, Planned Order Due Dates, and Planned Order Releases:

- The projected available balance is the projected available balance from the previous period, from which is deducted the gross requirement for that period, and to which is added the scheduled order receipts. Safety stock is not deducted from the projected available balance, but rather set as the minimum projected available balance to be maintained in the MRP netting process.
- The net requirement is the minimum quantity to be ordered set by the netting logic of the MRP system. The final net requirement generates a planned order. The planned order quantity is set by the item's order policy and lot-sizing rules.
- The planned order due date is determined by the date the items are required for manufacturing, and due dates for order-related actions are calculated backwards from this planned order due date to insure that it is met, one of which is the planned order release date. The planned order release date is set as one item lead time back from the planned order due date.

Safety Stock and Material Allocations

Safety stock is incorporated into MRP systems as the target minimum inventory for independent demand items. When the MRP calculations show that an independent demand item in stock will fall below its safety stock, a net requirement is created resulting in an order for the item being generated. For dependent demands within manufacturing, the concept of safety lead time is used instead of safety stock to protect against frequent and unnecessary order generation.

Material allocations are incorporated into MRP systems by adding them to the gross requirements for the first period, unless allocation over a set number of periods is specified. The projected available balance for the first period is then the on-hand balance added to the scheduled receipts and planned orders, from which is subtracted the gross requirements and allocations. In later periods the projected available balance will be the on-hand balance (also the projected available balance from the last period) added to the scheduled receipts and planned orders, from which is subtracted the gross requirements.

Generation of Time-Phased Requirements

Generating time-phased requirements is the third step of detailed material planning, and is simply calculating a materials ordering schedule that will enable the fulfillment of production requirements. The master production schedule (MPS) orders are entered into the MRP system as firm planned orders, which are then exploded through all levels of the bills of material to calculate the dependent requirements for raw materials and other components. These dependent requirements are compared against projected available stock to determine net requirements that in turn generate planned orders. Planned orders are re-classified as firm planned orders when due dates and quantities are confirmed by the planner, and re-classified again as scheduled receipts once the orders are placed or released as scheduled.

Material Plan Validity

Since the production environment and parameters are continually changing, an important consideration in materials planning is maintaining the validity of the plan. The detailed material planning process not only produces initial recommendations for scheduling orders, but also produces recommendations for re-planning orders as necessary in response to change in order to maintain a valid material schedule based on current priorities. Detailed material scheduling is an ongoing process, affected by changing demands and production. Maintaining the material plan's validity includes maintaining priorities, re-planning, revising planning parameters, and what-if analysis and modeling.

Maintaining Priorities

Along with re-planning, revising planning parameters, and what-if analysis and modeling, maintaining priorities is an important step in maintaining the material plan's validity. Maintaining priorities refers to keeping order priorities up to date based on changes in the demand priorities. Changes in demand priorities affect the inventory allocation as well as order timing, which in turn affect ordering priorities. Order priorities are maintained through priority planning, priority control, and a dispatching system (typically a daily dispatch list). Relative priority, absolute priority, priority integrity, actual lead time, planned lead time, and horizontal and vertical dependencies are all concepts related to maintaining priorities.

Re-Planning

Along with maintaining priorities, revising planning parameters, and what-if analysis and modeling, re-planning is an important step in maintaining the validity of the material plan. An important feature of material requirements planning (MRP) is continuous re-planning. Every time an MRP regeneration run is performed, the schedule is re-planned, and every time a net generation run is performed, the schedule is partially re-planned. Through bottom up re-planning, expediting, and de-expediting, all of which are components of re-planning, discrepancies that arise between the due dates and actual need dates for manufactured or purchased parts are dealt with and current material requirements and scheduling are realigned. Important concepts and processes related to re-planning include differentiation of due dates and need dates, rescheduling manufacturing orders and purchase orders, bottom up re-planning, expediting and de-expediting, and queue squeezing.

Maintaining Order Priorities

Maintaining order priorities terms:

- Priority planning: The determination of the required materials, their quantities and their scheduling to meet production goals using the tools master production scheduling and material requirements planning.
- Priority control: The execution of the schedule set by priority planning through communicating required tasks and their start and finish dates to manufacturing using a dispatching system.
- Dispatching system: The method for communicating the current priority plan to manufacturing, most commonly through a daily dispatch list.
- Daily dispatch list: A daily report produced by the dispatching system and issued to manufacturing work centers listing the jobs to be performed in order of priority, usually according to start or completion date.
- Relative priority: A manufacturing task's rating or where the manufacturing task falls on a prioritized list of manufacturing tasks to be performed.
- Absolute priority: The actual date on which a manufacturing task must be completed.
- Actual lead time: The length of time spent manufacturing a particular order; actual lead times are variable due to unanticipated material or capacity problems.
- Planned lead time: The anticipated length of time for production of an order calculated by the material requirements planning (MRP) system by summing the anticipated time spent being moved to and from processing, queuing for processing, setting up the process, running the process, and so on.
- Horizontal dependencies: The dependence of a part's required due date on other parts at the same level in the product structure; although an item due date may be initially set based solely on backwards logic from the master production schedule (MPS) target finished goods due date, the due date is not valid if the other components for manufacturing the parent part cannot be available then, and the due date will change accordingly to a time when all necessary materials can be available to begin production.
- Vertical dependencies: The dependence of a part's required due date on higher level demand, like its parent part's order release date or the master production schedule target finished goods date; component parts must be available in time for the parent part to be constructed by the parent's due date and for even higher level due dates to be met.

Dispatching System

To be effective, a dispatching system must incorporate several key characteristics. Manufacturing orders that meet production requirements must be generated and maintained, including the use of scheduling logic to establish task start and due dates. A daily dispatch list or other report must be produced and issued to manufacturing so that the scheduled orders are fulfilled. It is becoming more common for an online report reflecting up-to-the-minute changes in priorities to be available to manufacturing. Finally, the dispatching system must maintain order status and audit information, including tracking the order through the manufacturing process.

Priority Changes

Due to the fluid nature of the manufacturing environment, priority changes must sometimes be made. When materials or production capacity are unexpectedly unavailable, when product orders vary greatly from forecast demand, when actual lead times are significantly different from planned lead times, and when other unexpected changes occur the materials plan and corresponding priorities also change. It is possible for regeneration and/or or net generation runs of the MRP system to produce order release dates and/or due dates that are untenable or have even already passed. When this occurs, the system planner must consult with manufacturing to see if it is feasible to commit to the new schedule, if the manufacturing can "catch up" with the MRP order schedule.

An MRP system uses the master production schedule (MPS) in conjunction with the initial data to calculate a prioritized material plan. Priority integrity is the extent to which the prioritized plan is valid and feasible. If the initial data used by the MRP system is accurate and up-to-date then the calculated plan will be valid, meaning that the due dates are relevant and must be met in order to meet the MPS. If the scheduled order due dates and the actual required dates for those orders are far apart, manufacturing may well begin ignoring the schedule since it is not relevant for meeting MPS requirements. This situation can occur when planned lead times are too long or when changes occur without corresponding schedule changes. Beyond being valid, the scheduling must be feasible. Having a schedule that would meet MPS requirements does not help if the schedule cannot be met. The planner must be in contact with manufacturing about schedule feasibility, especially with regard to rescheduling.

Due and Need Dates

A due date is when a purchased or manufactured part is scheduled to be available to manufacturing, based on upstream manufacturing requirements derived from the master production schedule (MPS). The need date for the item is when it is actually needed in manufacturing for processing. Originally, an item's due date is set by the MRP system according to its manufacturing need date, so the two are the same or very close together. Over time changes occur such as unexpected demand fluctuations, late deliveries, manufacturing problems, etc., so the need date for items in manufacturing also change. Once orders have been confirmed or placed, the MRP system can no longer change the due dates automatically although the need dates that drove them are changing, so the two dates can drift apart. Part of the function of an MRP system is to prompt the scheduler to make the necessary changes to keep the item due dates relevant to the item need dates by generating appropriate rescheduling action messages.

Rescheduling Orders

As an MRP system re-calculates time-phased netting logic to check ordering needs, the material requirements are netted against the current inventory, scheduled receipts, and open orders to verify that items will be available as needed for manufacturing. If the system finds a future date when materials needed for production will not be available, it is called a projected inventory shortage. When projected inventory shortages are discovered, the system generates rescheduling action messages to prevent the shortages. The planner must then reschedule orders if possible. Three rescheduling methods that can be used when a straightforward rescheduling is not feasible due to time and material constraints are bottom-up rescheduling, expediting/de-expediting, and order queue squeezing.

Bottom-up Re-planning and Queue Squeezing

Bottom-up re-planning is the process of re-planning production and material orders based on the materials that are available, rather than solely on the master production schedule (MPS) requirements; the process is dependent on pegging data, and is performed by the system planner and not by the material requirements planning (MRP) system; bottom-up re-planning is useful in situations where there is an unexpected and insurmountable material constraint to determine what can be accomplished toward the goal with the constraint in place

Queue squeezing is the process of decreasing an item's lead time by decreasing its queue and wait time in manufacturing in order to meet rescheduled priorities; queue squeezing involves increasing an item's relative priority, and is also called queue compression and order crashing

Expediting and De-expediting

Expediting is the process of rushing materials through the manufacturing or ordering process faster than the normal lead times for the materials in order to meet rescheduled production requirements; materials being expedited have a high relative priority; expediting is also called stock chasing, and is usually overseen by a dedicated expediting department or an expediter who reports directly to the system planner

De-expediting is the opposite of expediting; de-expediting is decreasing the relative priority of an item and slowing its manufacturing or ordering process to the regular lead-time, and sometimes includes delaying its due date; de-expediting is often overlooked in manufacturing, but enables the success of expediting to meet current priorities

Revising Planning Parameters

It is of paramount importance that the data used by a material requirements planning (MRP) system is accurate and up-to-date. Companies, manufacturing, demand, and priorities all change over time, and the corresponding planning parameters must change as well. Planning parameters include lead times, safety stock quantities, safety lead times, lot-sizing methods, and scrap allowances. The MRP netting calculations depend on these parameters, so a valid material plan requires that these parameters be current and correct. All of the variables that affect these parameters must be understood and tracked to some extent, and there must be personnel clearly responsible for updating them.

MRP System Parameters

Lead Time

Both purchased and manufactured parts have lead times, and in both cases there are several components adding up to those lead times.

The total purchasing lead time includes planning, the purchase transaction, the vendor's order processing and filling, delivery, incoming inspection, and depositing the purchase in inventory. It is the buyer's responsibility to track and record these individual lead times so that he can fulfill his job buying the materials and seeing them into inventory in the lead time recorded in the MRP system.

The total manufacturing lead time includes planning, releasing goods into manufacturing, and the actual manufacturing lead time consisting of queuing, setting up, running, waiting, and moving. Although the system planner does not control these lead times, it is his responsibility to know them and update them within the MRP system. Lead times are a manufacturing performance measurement, and as such manufacturing operations often strive to reduce them. The planner must record lead time changes to keep the MRP data up-to-date and the material plan valid.

Safety Stock

Safety stock is usually held to guarantee finished goods availability to meet customer orders. If safety stock is calculated statistically, then the quantity depends on the variability in demand, the lead time, and the target service level. Statistical safety stock quantities must be re-calculated when any of these factors change. If safety stock quantity is set as the amount of material used in a particular time period, then the safety stock quantity must be reset every time the demand forecast changes. This method is less efficient than statistical safety stock because it ignores the material's demand pattern. In both cases it is the system planner who is responsible for updating the quantity of safety stock to be held in the MRP records.

Safety Lead Time and Scrap Allowance

Safety lead time is used to guarantee availability of production materials for manufacturing, and is based on supplier reliability. The buyer is responsible for tracking supplier performance and setting safety lead times accordingly.

Although scrap is undesirable and adds to the cost of manufacturing, it must be accounted for in material planning because it is a reality in production. If scrap is not accounted for in material planning, then there may not be enough material available to meet production demand. Although scrap is a production reality, it is constantly being minimized in a good production environment. The MRP system parameter scrap allowance must be kept up-to-date to reflect the changes in the scrap allowances.

Lot-Sizing Method

There are three lot-sizing methods typically used with MRP systems. These are the fixed order quantity, the agreed order quantity, and time period ordering methods. Since the average inventory is calculated by adding half of the order quantity to the safety stock, order lot sizing affects the average inventory held and thus the efficiency of the MRP system.

In the fixed order quantity method, a set number of items must always be ordered, regardless of demand for the items. Suppliers sometimes impose fixed order quantities, and there is not much a manufacturer can do about it. In the agreed order quantity method, as the name implies, a lot size is agreed upon. The agreed order quantity can be based on a calculation of the economic order quantity (EOQ), a vehicle load capacity, or other factors. Time period ordering methods include period order quantity and periodic ordering, in which the order quantity is set based on the number of parts required for production in particular time periods.

Decreasing Average Inventory

Decreasing average inventory while successfully meeting the demand for inventory increases the effectiveness of an MRP system. Since average inventory is dependent on the lot size of material orders, decreasing the order lot size also decreases average inventory. How to decrease order lot size depends on the lot-sizing technique in use. When a supplier sets a firm fixed order quantity, there is nothing a manufacturer can do to decrease average inventory through decreasing lot size. When the economic order quantity is the agreed order quantity, lot size can be reduced by decreasing manufacturing set-up costs or external order costs since the EOQ depends on these. Similarly, in periodic ordering decreasing set-up and/or ordering costs can reduce the order quantity.

What-if Analysis and Modeling

What-if analysis and modeling entail the strategies and tools the system planner uses to further understand possible alternatives available to him in the material planning process. It is looking into the future, mathematically, to see what could or would happen in different given situations under the different material planning possibilities, and using that information to choose among those possibilities. What-if analysis and modeling includes both simulation and modeling as specific tools. Modeling is mathematically representing a system in order to study and better understand its behavior. Simulation is using a model to predict the outcomes within a system under different operating characteristics and conditions.

MRP What-if Facility

MRPII is a system for planning all of a manufacturer's material resources. It is a logical extension of material requirements planning (MRP) incorporating operational planning, financial planning, and the what-if facility. Through what-if analysis, MRPII systems can create and compare multiple master production schedules (MPS) to choose the best solution for problems with overloading, scheduling, and unforeseen demand. Through simulation costing, MRPII systems analyze the effect of possible changes on the product cost. Simulation costing is particularly useful in analyzing effects of changes in labor wages, foreign exchange rates, and import duties.

Simulation

Simulation is the process of entering historical or representative data sets into a system model to learn how the model handles different input situations. Although MRP is generally thought of as a planning tool, it is also a simulator. An MRP system predicts the future, or calculates future outcome based on the input conditions. The system goes beyond simulation in that it also specifies steps to be taken to change conditions to guarantee a certain outcome. That is, it generates action messages for actions necessary to fulfill the master production schedule (MPS). An MRP system simulates inventory conditions and production requirements, the result of which can be used to make ordering, manufacturing, and financial decisions. Through simulation, an MRP system identifies possible future problems so they can be prevented.

Linear Programming

Linear programming is a mathematical technique for determination of maximum or minimum points on a linearly constrained linear function of variables. Within MRP, linear programming is used to make decisions regarding allocation of limited resources in order to meet specific goals, like maximum profit or minimum cost, while still meeting production requirements. Some specific examples of situations in which MRP linear programming would be useful include planning production to meet seasonal demand patterns and minimize related costs such as hiring and laying off personnel, worker overtime, subcontracting, and holding inventory; assigning production levels and warehouse-filling responsibilities in a multiple-plant, multiple-warehouse manufacturing environment; scheduling production of multiple items in one manufacturing work center to meet production demand, not exceed production capacity, and minimize carrying and set-up costs.

Modeling

A model is a mathematical representation of a system that describes the system and can be used to predict system behavior under different circumstances. Within MRP, a model is developed to describe the relationship between the costs or profits and the uncontrollable variable product demand as well as controllable variables like production rate changes, inventory balances, batch sizes, order release rules, and safety stock quantities. A system model allows the system to be studied, tested, evaluated, and compared to alternative systems before implementation. Any potential change can be put through a test run on the system model. This ability to see how changes would work without implementing the changes is an invaluable tool.

MATERIAL PLANNING

ADVANTAGES OF WHAT-IF ANALYSIS

Running simulations on system models to perform what-if analysis is an invaluable tool for making material planning decisions. Through thoroughly exhausting the simulation possibilities by repetition of random number generation, system behavior under myriad circumstances can be considered, as well as system trends. It is also possible to gain a deeper understanding of multiple viable alternatives in order to make a well-informed comparison when choosing between those alternatives. Simulation events occur at the same relative frequency as in actual manufacturing, and simulation event sequences have the same occurrence probability as in actual manufacturing. Both average system performance and the possible range of system performance are discovered. The short amount of computer time required for running a simulation on a system model can provide years of manufacturing information.

INTERACTION BETWEEN MATERIAL PLANNING AND OTHER MANUFACTURING SYSTEMS

Material planning does not occur in isolation, but in relationship with other planning and control subsystems in the manufacturing environment. It is from the business planning process that the master schedule and/or customer orders that drive material planning originate. In response to this demand, the material planning determines lower level demand for items to meet production needs which in turn drive purchasing and/or production of materials. Through capacity planning the production capacity availability is checked against overall and lower level demands to verify viability of the plan and make appropriate changes if necessary.

RELATIONSHIP BETWEEN MATERIAL PLANNING AND BUSINESS PLANNING

Business planning, through sales and operations planning, sets the forecast finished goods demand and/or considers actual customer orders to develop a master schedule. The master schedule sets forth finished goods quantity and date requirements. It is this master schedule from the business planning process that drives material planning and material requirements planning (MRP) systems. Business planning provides the overall demand through the master schedule, whose derivative material quantity, time, and priority requirements comprise the master production schedule (MPS) requirements, which are met through material planning. The two processes together form the manufacturing demand and supply loop. In relationship to business planning, material planning must meet the specific lower level needs in number, date, and priority to fulfill the MPS. To fulfill the MPS requirements, the master scheduler, and material requirements planning (MRP) system rely on input from several demand sources, including the master schedule, the final assembly schedule, engineering data and planning data. All of this information is assimilated into and accounted for in the material plan.

INTERNAL INTERACTIONS WITHIN DETAILED SCHEDULING AND PLANNING

It is through the internal interactions within detailed scheduling and planning between material planning and capacity planning that the material plan requirements and production capacity for internally manufactured parts are reconciled. The material plan specifies dates, quantities, and priorities of parts required to meet the master schedule, but availability of the internally manufactured parts depends on the production capacity for those parts. The master scheduler uses the master schedule, which provides finished goods quantity and date requirements, to propose a master production schedule (MPS). In the MPS material requirements and dates are broken down through all levels of manufacturing scheduling all parts by item number, quantity, and date. It is through rough-cut capacity planning that the MPS is evaluated for feasibility, comparing requirements for internally produced parts to production capacity for those parts. Material requirements planning (MRP) is the input driving capacity requirements planning (CRP), and at the same time CRP acts as a limit on MRP.

INTERACTIONS BETWEEN MATERIAL PLANNING AND EXECUTION AND CONTROL

Material requirements planning (MRP) produces planned orders to meet master production schedule (MPS) requirements, which in turn, if filled, enable manufacturing to meet the finished goods requirements set forth by the master schedule. It is through execution and control that purchased parts for manufacturing are ordered and received. MRP produces planned orders, which the planner verifies and confirms. Once the order, including both quantity and timing, is confirmed, the order is released to the buyer in execution and control for completion. The buyer must choose a supplier and settle a price. Even after the order has been placed, MRP continually updates material requirements and the corresponding material plan, and may generate order rescheduling messages, which are handled like the original ordering messages.

ABC CLASSIFICATION

ABC classification is the process of organizing inventory materials into three, sometimes four, categories based on past or projected annual dollar volume (the item's annual usage multiplied by item cost) or other criteria. The three classes are labeled A, highest volume; B; and C, lowest volume. Sometimes a fourth class labeled D is used for obsolete and other non-moving items. The ABC classification system is used to differentiate inventory procedures and policies among the different classes of inventory items. Different amounts of attention and control are paid to and exercised over the different material classes, with more attention and tighter control specified for class A, descending through class C or D. ABC classification can be used specifically to set exception reporting, inventory cycle counting, and other inventory handling policies and procedures.

Bill of material example:

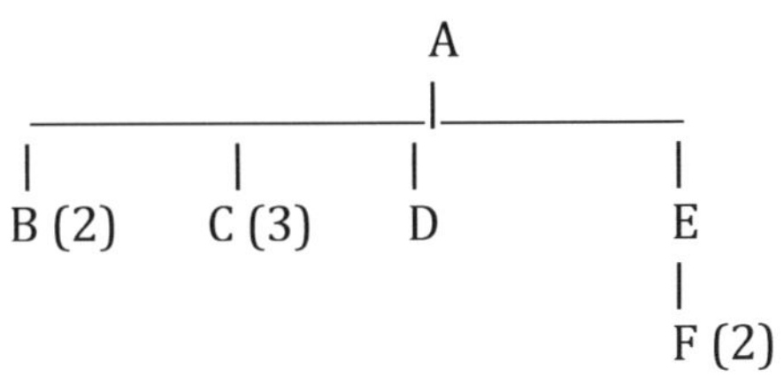

This multi-level bill of material for item A shows that item A is a parent part comprised of component parts B, C, D, and E. Through the manufacturing process, item A is fabricated from two item B's, three item C's, one item D and one item E. A single level bill of material would only include these two lines of information, and the assembly information for item E would have to be found in the bill of material for item E. Since this is a multi-level bill of material, the item E breakdown is included. Item E is a component part for item A and also a parent part constructed from two item F's.

PRODUCT STRUCTURE RECORDS EXAMPLE

Parent Part	Component Part	Quantity of Components per Parent	Scrap Factor
A	B	1	0
Parent Part	**Component Part**	**Quantity of Components per Parent**	**Scrap Factor**
A	C	3	0.1

The two product structure records are for items B and C, component parts of the parent part item A. The product structure record for component B shows that one item B is used to build parent part A. From the scrap factor of zero we know that it is anticipated that no item B's will be lost or damaged in assembly of the parent A. Similarly, from the product structure record for part C, it is known that three part C's are used to build part A, and ten percent of the C's are anticipated lost in the process.

Phantom Bill of Material

Phantom bill of material is a bill of material describing an item which is produced but not held in stock; these items are typically built as needed and consumed in manufacturing right away; material requirements planning (MRP) uses phantom bills of material to break down component needs for the material schedule, and can net against any that are held in stock although this is rare; phantom bills of material can also be called pseudo bills of material.

Allocation and Ordering Cost

Allocation is the process of breaking down the costs to the manufacturer of producing an item and attributing those costs to their different sources (in accounting); the process of assigning available inventory to be used to fill demand in production or customer orders (in inventory).

Ordering *cost* is the price for the process of acquiring goods from external sources, excluding the price for the goods themselves; ordering costs include costs incurred through order preparation, release, and monitoring as well as order receiving, handling, and inspection, and all associated clerical and administrative activities; the ordering cost is used to calculate order quantities, and can also be called the acquisition cost.

Important Terms

Backlog: Outstanding or open orders; all customer orders received and accepted by the company but not yet shipped to the customers, including back orders, current orders, and future orders.

Cellular layout: Manufacturing configuration based on work cells rather than work centers; work cells are groupings of machines and processes into a cell for producing a particular type of part or several different parts with similar resource requirements; work cells are considered as a single unit in the work center file and the routing sheet, rather than as individual work centers.

Cost of service: The financial cost associated with customer service; higher customer service levels extract higher costs; cost of service is comprised primarily of the cost of inventory necessary to maintain the desired service level.

Eighty-twenty rule: Pareto principle concept based on the idea that most results, effects, output, production, sales, costs, etc., result from just a few causes or sources, specifically that 20% of the possible causes produce 80% of the effects; the eighty-twenty rule is used in ABC classification where category A consists of the causative 20%.

Engineering data: Information describing the parts, part quantities, relationships between parts, production processes, process sequences, and associated timing through which the final product or intermediate assembly is manufactured; engineering data is used for overall inventory and production planning purposes, and consists of bills of material (BOM), routing data, and work center data.

EOQ=1: The condition of the economic order quantity being one, which means that batch sizes of one are economically feasible; EOQ=1 is an ideal to strive for through decreasing setup time and inventory.

Functional layout: Manufacturing configuration based on work centers.

Lead time: The amount of time required for completion of a specified action.

Manufacturing instruction: Detailed directions for workers processing parts; basic instructions can be included in the route sheet, but more complex instructions are contained in associated manufacturing instructions.

Manufacturing lead time: The amount of time required for completion of manufacturing, assuming that all necessary production materials are available for use; manufacturing lead time begins with release of raw materials into production and ends with storage or shipping of accepted finished goods.

Normal distribution: A statistical distribution of values that looks like the bell curve when graphed because values typically fall close to the average value, and are equally likely to be above or below the mean value.

Operation number: A number assigned to a factory process for identification purposes and that may be referenced in route sheets.

Parent part: A component part, intermediate assembly, or final product (parent) made from raw materials, component parts, intermediate assemblies or other materials (children); a part that is made from other parts is the parent part to those other parts.

Post-operation time: Necessary non-productive time after processing ends before moving to the next stage for recovery or finalization purposes such as cooling the part or allowing paint to dry.

Pre-operation time: Necessary non-productive time before a process begins specified in the routing sheet, for preparation purposes such as warming up equipment.

Product structure: The process flow for a parent part, including constituent parts, their quantities, and how they are put together to form the parent.

Product structure record: A computerized record of the product structure detailing the relationship of a part to its parent; all parts used to produce a parent part have a product structure record detailing the relationship to the parent and other related information.

Purchasing lead time: The amount of time required for completion of a material purchase, including order preparation, order placement, supplier lead time, delivery time, and raw materials receipt, inspection, acceptance, and storage in inventory

Quality: The extent to which a product conforms to the customer's specifications; usability

Random variation: Deviation in values due to random, unknown, or uncertain causes.

Responsiveness: A company's ability or lack thereof to meet a customer's needs in a timely fashion; a central component of responsiveness is manufacturing lead time; methods for increasing responsiveness include adopting the just-in-time model, and maintaining inventory of semi-finished goods so that they can be finished and shipped when an order is received, rather than manufactured from the first step when the order is received.

Routing: An item's pathway through manufacturing, including manufacturing processes, the order of manufacturing processes, the labor and equipment required for each process, instructions for the process operators, the rate at which the processes are performed including process set-up times, and any associated specifications.

Routing file: A record of the routing for a product; routing files include operation numbers, work centers, descriptions, set-up times, item run times, and type of labor for each process, and may also include pre-operation time, post-operation time, any additional text to be included, and tool numbers to be used; the routing file is also called the route sheet.

Safety factor: The number of standard deviations or mean average deviations (MAD) necessary to insure the desired customer service level; the safety factor is looked up in a table of safety factors for normal distribution based on the desired service level and then used to calculate the amount of safety stock necessary.

Scrap: Materials that are found to be outside material specifications and for which rework is not feasible; nonconforming materials.

Scrap factor: A percentage of an item used in a particular production process to compensate for expected loss of the item during that production process; the scrap factor only applies when the item is used in the manufacturing process to which the scrap factor applies, thus the scrap factor is recorded in the product structure.

Scrap quantity: A fixed number of parts that is expected to be lost in every run of a particular manufacturing operation, typically as part of the set-up or end of the process.

Seasonality: A demand cycle of varying highs and lows that is repeated per time period.

Shrinkage factor: A percentage of an item inventory balance that is used to compensate for expected losses of the item during manufacturing; the shrinkage factor applies to the item regardless of the production process and thus is recorded in the item master record; shrinkage factors are also called scrap percentages.

Single-level where used: A report describing a manufacturing component in which all of the component's parent parts are detailed, along with the quantity of the component used in each parent part.

Stock out: The situation in which a particular inventory item has run out; a finished goods stock out can lead to lost sales, loss of customer good will, costs incurred to purchase substitutes, etc.

Stock out percentage: The percentage of orders or order line items that result in a stock out in a given time period; the stock out percentage is a quantitative measure of a company's ability to fill orders.

Tool number: Number assigned to tools for identification purposes and that may be referenced in route sheets.

Trend: The general tendency of a value changing over time, either upward or downward.

Work center: The physical manufacturing location where a process occurs, indicated as a code on the route sheet, containing one or more workers and/or machines.

Work center data: Information related to work centers, specifically their capacity, planning, and control information.

Work center file: A record of work center data used for planning purposes.

Yield: The percentage of process input items that are manufactured into usable output items.

Lead-Time Fixed Data Terms

Cumulative lead time: The amount of time required for the completion of finished goods when no stock is available for use; cumulative lead time is the sum of the manufacturing and purchasing lead times.

MRP lead-time offset: Technique within an MRP system for determining an order date based on subtracting the purchasing lead time for external orders and manufacturing lead time for internal orders from the target delivery date.

Low level coding: The process used in MRP systems of assigning numbers to items in order to indicate the lowest level bills of material on which the items appear; this number prevents the MRP system from completing netting logic on the item until all demands for the item have been tallied.

Inventory Data Terms

Stock on hand: The materials currently held in a company's inventory; material requirements planning (MRP) systems commonly allow for inclusion of items in multiple storage locations in its stock on hand records; stock on hand is also called inventory balance, current stock, or balance on hand.

Open orders: Requisitions for goods from an external supplier or from internal manufacturing which have not yet been received or filled, orders which have been placed but not yet received; open orders are also called stock on order.

Scheduled receipts: Orders that have been placed with an external supplier or internal manufacturing, setting an anticipated delivery date; MRP status for an order once it has been placed but not yet received.

Requirements Data Terms

Requirement records: Information about the demand for individual component parts created by the MRP system when a planned order is created for a parent part, including component item number, parent item number, the quantity of the item necessary for constructing the parent, the order number, and the order completion target date; the actual requirement for the component part is calculated by multiplying the number of parent parts to be produced by the number of components used in manufacturing the parent, with an allowance for scrap added in.

Gross requirements: Demand for parts that exist before netting, generated by customer orders, forecasting, and upper level requirements.

Material allocations: An MRP status assigned to inventory materials that have been requested but not yet released into production; material allocations are necessary since the items are no longer available for other uses although they are still in inventory; material allocations prevent MRP systems from using unavailable inventory as available inventory in calculations.

Planning Operations to Support the Priority Plan

Production Capacity Scheduling

Production capacity scheduling, or simply capacity scheduling, is the process of planning internal production capability to meet the requirements of the master production schedule (MPS). Capacity scheduling includes assessing available internal production resources, their supporting activities, and any constraints on either and balancing these against the material plan to determine a production plan. In addition to having the appropriate materials available when needed, meeting MPS and master schedule requirements requires sufficient production capacity to be available to manufacture the products on time. Capacity scheduling is typically accomplished through capacity requirements planning (CRP) and is also called operations planning.

Capacity Requirements Planning

Capacity requirements planning (CRP) is a specific tool used by the system planner to plan production capacity. The system planner uses CRP to schedule manufacturing using MRP-generated orders. The orders are broken down into individual manufacturing operations. The quantity of items ordered is multiplied by the standard item run time for each operation to determine the capacity required to complete the order. The required capacity is then compared to the available capacity, and manufacturing operations are scheduled accordingly to produce the capacity requirements plan. CRP systems do not typically produce action messages like MRP systems, but rather maintain status reports. The status reports are usually summarized as histograms or percentage load reports to streamline the information.

Units of Measure

The units of measure used in capacity planning vary greatly between industries, as well as between levels of manufacturing. For example, units of measure discussed in a board meeting may be millions of dollars or tons, while a detailed scheduling and planning meeting would focus on standard work hours or units of production. Within a manufacturing environment, there must be a universal measurement applicable to all products and processes that can be used for planning purposes. If all items produced in a plant consume similar resources at similar rates, then units of production can be the common unit of measure. In most cases, however, standard work hours are the common unit of measure that can be used to bring all processes and products to a common base. In most manufacturing resource planning (MRPII) systems, standard work hours are used as the default unit of measure for capacity requirements calculations.

Period Size

The material requirements planning (MRP) process, which provides the input into the capacity requirements planning (CRP) process, is usually performed with a period size of one day, while CRP is usually performed with a period size of one hour. In CRP system reports, several days can be grouped together into one time period. There is much variation between calculation and report period sizes. These differences pose a scheduling problem when manufacturing operations are short and more than one can be performed in a day. Some manufacturing resource planning (MRPII) systems allow the scheduling of more than one process per day, but in most cases manual input by the system planner is necessary to manage the timing and sequencing of multiple operations in one day.

Production Environment

There are many aspects of production that together comprise the production environment. The types of products a company manufactures, the volume of products manufactured, the finished goods handling employed, the management philosophy, the manufacturing methods, and the factory lay-out are all production environment factors and as such affect detailed capacity planning. Although the basic capacity planning requirements are always the same, production environment factors affect the relative importance of the capacity planning requirements within that manufacturing system. In particular, the finished goods handling method (make-to-stock, make-to-order, or mixed) as well as the type of production (job shop, repetitive manufacture, or process manufacture) exert a strong influence on the operation of material requirements planning (MRP) and capacity requirements planning (CRP).

Make-to-Order Manufacturing

There are four approaches commonly used by make-to-order companies, differentiated by the step in the manufacturing flow where specialization begins. The first approach is customizing to order, which simply consists of make-to-stock production with standard finished goods being individually customized according to customer orders. The second approach is assemble-to-order production, in which standard components, modules, and subassemblies are stocked and used to assemble a particular final product when a customer order is received. Assemble-to-order is sometimes considered its own category alongside make-to-order. The third approach is manufacturing to order, in which companies maintain stores of raw materials and piece parts that are manufactured into products in response to customer orders. The fourth approach includes engineering to order and entails even specialized ordering. These make-to-order companies specialize from the very beginning. Raw materials and piece parts for production are not ordered until a customer order for finished goods is received.

Types of Production

There are three types of production: job shop, repetitive manufacture, and process manufacture. The type of production utilized within a company depends on the quantity of manufactured parts required and the company's management philosophy. More than one type of production can be used concurrently. If demand for a particular part is very high, a company will likely choose repetitive manufacture for that part by setting up a dedicated assembly line. Low-demand parts typically share manufacturing resources in a job shop operation. A recent trend in manufacturing is the just-in-time philosophy, which is heavily dependent on the commitment level of management.

Repetitive and Process Manufacture

Both repetitive manufacture and process manufacture entail dedicated production facilities, unlike job shop operations in which a large variety of products can be produced. In repetitive manufacture, the fixed product assembly line has balanced work centers working at a fixed rate; materials from suppliers, stock, and lower levels of production are issued through back flushing and are fed directly into the assembly line in a flow approach; and the main assembly line is usually scheduled according to finite capacity loading while feeder assembly lines are scheduled according to infinite capacity loading. Like repetitive manufacture, process manufacturing facilities are structured according to the actual manufacturing steps for the product. Process manufacturing can be performed in batch or continuous mode; lot sizes are determined by equipment limitations like vessel and pipe sizes; set-ups are required, usually for the purpose of cleaning between products; finite capacity loading is usually employed; and routing is fixed.

ISSUES OF CAPACITY

BETWEEN RATED AND DEMONSTRATED CAPACITY

Capacity, the maximum production capability of a machine, process, assembly line, facility, etc., can be determined in different ways. The rated capacity is the capacity that is calculated through industrial engineering. Not only can capacity be calculated, it can also be measured. Measured capacity is known as demonstrated capacity, and is simply the actual, physically demonstrated production capability.

BALANCING LOAD AND CAPACITY

Balancing the load and capacity in a production environment is simply establishing the required load for the time period under consideration, establishing the available capacity for that time period, comparing the two and planning accordingly. If the load is less than the available capacity, additional load can be added for the period, or the period can be under planned. Under planning manufacturing is simply not loading to full capacity. If the load is the same as the capacity, the production requirements will be met, but no additional load can be added without delaying work or temporarily increasing capacity. If the load is greater than the capacity, then some production must be delayed to a later period or capacity must be temporarily increased.

UNDERPLANNING

Under planning, loading manufacturing below its capacity, is a strategy used by some companies to improve their customer service. When a manufacturing system is under loaded, manufacturing wait time is decreased, improving workflow and decreasing overall throughput time. This in turn shortens customer response time and improves customer service. In short, the flexibility provided by under planning manufacturing can give a company a competitive advantage in meeting customer needs. Capacity can be increased temporarily using several methods, including worker overtime, reallocation of workers to increase personnel temporarily at the process in question, subcontracting the required work that exceeds capacity outside of the facility, and alternate routing within the facility for production.

TECHNIQUES FOR LOAD AND CAPACITY BALANCING

In the process of balancing manufacturing load and capacity, there are two primary considerations. These considerations are the actual loading of a manufacturing system or work center, and scheduling these assigned loads. Typically, loading is assigned through either an infinite loading or finite loading framework. Most material requirements planning (MRP) systems use infinite loading as the default framework for assigning manufacturing load. There are three finite loading techniques: process-oriented finite loading, order-oriented finite loading, and constraint-oriented finite loading. The manufacturing load is generally scheduled using the backward or forward scheduling method, but there are also alternative scheduling methods such as central point scheduling and probable scheduling.

INSUFFICIENT MANUFACTURING CAPACITY

When the available manufacturing capacity is not sufficient to meet production requirements, there are several options available. The capacity can be increased temporarily, the portion of required work not covered by the available capacity can be delayed, or the entire order can be delayed. The delays entail changing the order completion date. Capacity may not be sufficient for the required load in a backward scheduling framework. It is possible that backward scheduling can schedule operations to start in the past in order to meet required completion dates, but this is impossible.

Operation Scheduling and Loading

Operation scheduling is the process of calculating operation start and end dates for each individual operation required to fill a work order. Through the process of operation scheduling, operation dates are set and operations are sequenced within work centers based on the operation dates. Inputs required to schedule operations are up-to-date material requirements planning (MRP) order quantities and due dates, routing for all parent parts, work center data, and the moving time between operations. Operation scheduling is particularly effective in production environments driven by work orders or characterized by complex and variable product routings or sequencing rules affecting when jobs can be done.

Infinite and Finite Loading

Infinite loading is a method for balancing manufacturing load and capacity in which, mathematically, load is assumed to be infinite and thus assigned without regard for capacity. Finite loading is a method for balancing manufacturing load and capacity in which assigning load is limited by known, finite capacity; finite loading can be process-oriented, order-oriented, or constraint-oriented

Forward and Backward Scheduling

Forward scheduling is the process of scheduling operations based on the process start dates, the dates when the orders are released into manufacturing; the completion dates are then determined by adding the operation lead times to the start date; forward scheduling operates with a fixed start date but flexible end date. Backward scheduling is the process of scheduling operations base on the required completion date, the date when the items must be available for higher level manufacturing; the start date is determined by subtracting the operation lead times from the completion dates; backward scheduling operates with a fixed end date but flexible start date

Forward Scheduling with Finite Loading

Forward scheduling with finite loading is a technique for balancing manufacturing load and capacity in which scheduling is based on required start dates using a known finite manufacturing capacity. The start date is the day that material is released into production. From that day, the manufacturing system is loaded to the known finite capacity until the order is complete. The time it takes to manufacture the required quantity using the available capacity sets the flexible end date when the items will be available to upper level manufacturing or released into finished goods inventory.

Backward Scheduling with Finite Loading

Backward scheduling with finite loading is a technique for balancing manufacturing load and capacity in which scheduling is based on required completion dates using a known finite manufacturing capacity. The completion date is the day that the items must be available for higher levels of production. From that day, manufacturing is scheduled backward by loading the manufacturing system to capacity to meet the completion date. This backward loading sets the flexible start date needed in order to meet the completion date. If there are multiple requirements, planning begins with the requirement farthest into the future and manufacturing operations are loaded backward sequentially from that point to meet the multiple requirements.

Forward Scheduling and Backward Scheduling with Infinite Loading

Forward scheduling with infinite loading is a technique for balancing manufacturing load and capacity in which scheduling is based on required start dates, working forward in time from those start dates while assuming infinite manufacturing capacity. The flexible completion date is set by adding the manufacturing lead time to the start date. Backward scheduling with infinite loading is a technique for balancing manufacturing load and capacity in which scheduling is based on required end dates, working backward in time from those end dates while assuming infinite manufacturing capacity. The manufacturing lead time is subtracted from the required completion date to set the flexible start date. Material requirements planning (MRP) systems typically use backward scheduling with infinite loading. In forward scheduling and backward scheduling with infinite loading, manufacturing capacity is not considered in setting the schedule since capacity is assumed to be infinite. In both cases it is necessary for the system planner to orchestrate detailed loading to provide a balanced workload to manufacturing.

Planned and Released Load

Load, the production actually assigned or released to manufacturing, can be classified as planned load or released load. The planned load is future planned production determined by material requirements planning (MRP) logic. The released load is the actual work orders already released into manufacturing.

Time Phasing Load

Material requirements planning (MRP) produces material requirements with completion dates. The completion date is when the item must be available to be released into manufacturing. The capacity requirements planning (CRP) process considers the capacity necessary to produce the required parts. The required production is broken down into the individual operations specified in the material routing, and each individual operation's load is calculated by added the operation set-up time to the product of the number required and the unit run time. CRP determines timing starting with the MRP required completion date. CRP works backward from the completion date through the time required for each sequential operation, including queuing, waiting, moving, setting up and running, to schedule the operations. Once the operations are scheduled, then required load per work center per time period corresponding to the master production schedule (MPS) can be calculated and reported.

MRPII Weaknesses

In the past, the weakest points of MRPII have been capacity management and execution. This is currently changing. One key to improving capacity management and execution within MRPII is using more than one load and capacity balancing technique in conjunction, rather than choosing only one. Using these tools together provides better manufacturing simulation from which to schedule actual manufacturing. Beyond using load and capacity balancing techniques in conjunction, capacity management and execution is improving because of new MRPII add-on modules such as linear and non-linear mathematical models. These models are used to determine how to achieve maximum profit, minimum cost, or some other objective through allocating limited resources. Linear mathematical models apply to linear functions, while non-linear mathematical models apply to non-linear functions.

Constraint and Bottleneck

Constraint is the limiting factor, either physical or procedural, that caps the performance or throughput of a manufacturing system. Bottleneck is a work center that acts as a physical constraint on a manufacturing system; bottlenecks are usually work centers through which most orders are processed and are often delayed. Theory of Constraints (TOC) is a production management philosophy based on the idea that a manufacturing system consists of several sequential parts, one of which constrains the system from meeting its goal; TOC is divided into logistics, performance measurement, and logical thinking and focuses on removing the constraint.

CONSTRAINT IDENTIFICATION AND MANAGEMENT

Since constraints are the limiting factors on production output, they actually limit the business itself. Bottlenecks in particular set the production rate for all parts that go through them, and thus the production rate for the whole system. It is of paramount importance to identify these system constraints and manage them well to maximize production and business output. Some steps that can be taken to keep bottlenecks producing smoothly include continuous operation of the work center by double staffing and staggering meals and breaks for workers, advance preparation of batches arriving for production at the work center, alternate routing and subcontracting as much of the work as possible, and classification of work center maintenance and repair as top priority for maintenance personnel.

BOTTLENECK AND ITS FEEDER WORK CENTER

The bottleneck's feeder work center is the process immediately prior to the bottleneck work center, the one that feeds it material for processing. In drum-buffer-rope scheduling, an inventory buffer of input materials is maintained from the feeder work center to input into the bottleneck work center to insure continuous production at the bottleneck. The quantity of materials held in the inventory buffer depends on the relationship between the bottleneck and its feeder, particularly their production capacities. If the feeder greatly exceeds the bottleneck in production capacity, then the buffer can be small since it can be restocked quickly after depletion, but if the capacity difference between the bottleneck and its feeder is small, then the buffer must be large since it cannot be restocked quickly after depletion.

DRUM, BUFFER, ROPE SCHEDULING

Drum is the rate of production set for a manufacturing system by the system's constraint. Buffer is inventory maintained to input into the bottleneck work center so that production continues even when there are problems upstream; the amount of the buffer is dependent on the capacity difference between the constraining work center and the work center that feeds it. Rope is the process of communication between the bottleneck point and the material release point to insure that no more material is released into production than can be handled by the constraining work center.

Drum-buffer-rope scheduling is a production management technique in which manufacturing throughput is maximized by identifying the system constraint or bottleneck and pacing the manufacturing system by the constraint work rate, providing buffer inventory to keep the bottleneck producing, and limiting material release into production by real-time communication with the bottleneck.

CRP CALCULATIONS

In order to make the necessary calculations to compare system loading and available capacity, a CRP system needs the demand for products, established work centers, the product routings, and the required manufacturing times. The product demand by time period is supplied by the material requirements planning (MRP) process as planned orders and scheduled receipts. The manufacturing load fulfills these product orders. Manufacturing facilities need to be broken down into work centers for scheduling purposes. The work centers through which a product is processed are specified on the product routings and used to break the manufacturing order down into individual operations. Product routings are necessary for all manufactured parts used to fulfill the orders in question. Required manufacturing times such as set-up and run times enable CRP to establish the time required for individual operations.

CRP Load Versus Capacity Report

The output of the CRP process is simply the comparison information between system load and capacity. One typical format is the load versus capacity summary report. The load versus capacity report details the released load, planned load, total load (released load plus planned load), available capacity, amount over or under capacity (available capacity minus the total load), and cumulative amount over or under capacity (sum of amounts over or under capacity up till that time period) by time period, including an initial past due time period. The load versus capacity report is formatted as a table of information. Requests for load versus capacity reports must specify the time horizon to be included, or the entire CRP horizon is used. The system planner uses the cumulative amount over or under capacity as a guideline for detailed scheduling and planning. Loads over capacity can be rescheduled into previous time periods with loads under capacity if possible, or the planner can negotiate with manufacturing to increase capacity to meet production requirements.

CRP Percentage Load Report

The output of the CRP process is simply the comparison information between system load and capacity. One typical format is the percentage load report. The percentage load report lists the percentage load, which is the percentage of available capacity consumed by the assigned load, by time period, including an initial past due time period. In addition to the percentage load list is a list including actual load by time period, total load, average load per time period, and average percent load per time period. Averages per time period do not include the initial past due time period. The system planner uses the information in the report to regulate any imbalances manually.

Process Flow Manufacturing

Process flow manufacturing is a production environment in which interruptions to actual processing runs and groups of processing runs of similar products are minimized by equating the process flow and the flow of material through production. In process flow manufacturing queue time, operating costs, and inventory are minimized while production throughput and customer service are maximized.

Process Flow Scheduling

Process flow scheduling is the process of scheduling process flow manufacturing. This scheduling is based on the process structure rather than product routings as in a job shop environment or product structure as in a material requirements planning (MRP) environment. For the purposes of process flow scheduling, a manufacturing facility is comprised of a network of process units, clusters, stages, and trains. Processor-dominated or material dominated scheduling logic is used to schedule process clusters, and reverse flow scheduling, forward flow scheduling, or mixed flow scheduling logic is used to schedule process trains.

Types of Process Flow Scheduling

- Processor-dominated scheduling: A process flow scheduling technique used to schedule process clusters in which the equipment is scheduled before material availability is verified because of a well-defined capacity limitation; processor-dominated scheduling sets low-cost process sequences and economic run lengths.
- Material-dominated scheduling: A process flow scheduling technique used to schedule process clusters in which material is scheduled before availability of production capacity is verified; in material-dominated scheduling, scheduling for one cluster is finalized before beginning scheduling for the next cluster; material-dominated scheduling minimizes inventory holding since receipts are scheduled to occur as they are needed for production.

- Reverse flow scheduling: A process flow scheduling technique used to schedule process trains in which the final process stage is scheduled first, and then working backwards through the process structure to the first process stage.
- Forward flow scheduling: A process flow scheduling technique used to schedule process trains in which the initial process stage is scheduled first, and then working sequentially through the process structure to the final process stage.
- Mixed flow scheduling: A process flow scheduling technique used to schedule process trains in which the critical or bottleneck process is scheduled first, proceeding sequentially to the final process stage and backwards to the initial process stage from the critical point; mixed flow scheduling can also be called inside-out scheduling.

Process Flow Scheduling Terms

- Process unit: Processing equipment and/or machines that are grouped together and share the same schedule.
- *Process cluster*: Sequential process unit(s) that are grouped together because one feeds completely and directly into the next; process clusters do not share the same schedule because they perform different functions, but their schedules are coupled together because of the direct feeding from one process unit to the next within the cluster.
- Process stage: Process clusters that are grouped together but separated from previous and subsequent process stages by inventories; there is not a complete and direct feed between the process stages, so the schedules are neither the same nor coupled.
- Process train: Sequential process stages that are grouped together because they can be scheduled independently from other process trains
- Process flow analysis: The practice of detailing the production paths of manufactured goods within a process flow manufacturing environment and using this information to improve the process flow; it is through process flow analysis that process trains are determined.
- Flow process chart: An elementary yet thorough depiction of the series of actions comprising a process including all required individual actions, detailed inter-operational actions, classification of actions as value-added or non-value-added, and the total times per action; more simply, a flow process chart is a diagram of the process flow with associated information.

CRP Necessary Information

The information necessary to perform CRP calculations is the routing data for products being produced and the work center data for processes being performed. The information is used to schedule manufacturing orders and assign manufacturing load to work centers by time period. The material requirements plan is used along with the product routing data to establish manufacturing order release and completion dates, which in turn serve as the basis for loading manufacturing. Work center efficiency and utilization data determines the rated capacity, which limits the capacity available for loading.

The product routing file or route sheet includes operation numbers, work centers, descriptions of work performed, set-up times, unit run times, and labor grades. Pre-operation times, post-operation times, discretionary text, tool numbers, and manufacturing instructions may also be included. The work center file includes work center number, capacity information, alternate work centers available, efficiency and utilization data, and queue time. Work center files describe either individual work centers (functional layout) or groups of work centers called work cells (cellular layout).

WORK CENTER TERMS

- Efficiency: A calculation of the planned standard hours for a manufacturing job divided by the actual hours required to accomplish the job for a particular work center, usually expressed as a percentage; a work center's efficiency is used to determine its rated capacity, and also serves as a performance measure.
- Utilization: A calculation of the number of hours actually worked divided by the number of hours available for work by personnel and/or machines comprising a work center, usually expressed as a percentage; a work center's utilization is used to determine its rated capacity, and served historically as a work center's primary performance measure but has now been replaced by on-time schedule completion in that role.
- Alternate work center: Another work center specified in the work center file which can be used for the same production if the work center under consideration is overloaded; alternative work centers must be chosen by the system planner through a manual override since they are not part of the capacity requirements planning (CRP) process.

SYSTEM CAPACITY THEORY

The production capacity of a manufacturing system can be defined theoretically through a brute force calculation of the system's maximum possible output. This calculation is simply the product of the number of process machines or personnel, the number of hours per shift, and the number of shifts per time period (usually daily). No allowance is made for maintenance, repairs, shutdowns, breaks or other down time. Since no allowances are made for any manufacturing delays or unproductive time, the theoretical capacity is impossible to achieve and an impractical guideline for loading manufacturing. Demonstrated capacity, which is also called *measured or actual capacity*, is the manufacturing system's historical output per time period (usually in standard hours per day). Since the demonstrated capacity consists of what the system can actually do and has been doing, it should be used as the system capacity for loading manufacturing. The system will continue to produce the demonstrated capacity unless the production environment changes, in which case the capacity must be adjusted accordingly.

RATED CAPACITY

SYSTEM CAPACITY RATED DEFINITION

Rated capacity, which is also called calculated, nominal or standing capacity, is usually calculated by the industrial engineering or engineering design departments using work center data. The rated capacity is the product of the work center's available hours, utilization and efficiency. In the Theory of Constraints (TOC), this formula changes slightly. TOC rated capacity is the product of the work center's available hours, efficiency and activation. In TOC available hours refers to all of the time the machine is literally available and fit to be used and not just the worker time scheduled, and activation refers to the number of hours the machine is needed for scheduled production. The rated capacity and demonstrated capacity should be close to each other. If they are not, either the rated capacity has been incorrectly calculated or something is wrong in the system that must be identified and corrected.

UTILIZATION AND EFFICIENCY

The efficiency, a percentage of the standard hours planned for a manufacturing system to perform a task divided by the actual time the manufacturing system takes to perform the task, is a measure of how well the system is operating. Efficiency percentages can be over one hundred if the system performs more quickly than planned. The higher the efficiency, the better the system is operating. The utilization, a percentage of the hours a system is actually working to the system's available hours is a measurement of the system's usage level. Percent utilization is between zero and one hundred. Both the efficiency and utilization are factors, expressed as ratios rather than percentages, in calculating a system's rated capacity.

Manufacturing Load Sources

In general, manufacturing load comes primarily from planned orders, firm planned orders, and scheduled receipts. Manufacturing requirements planning (MRP) generates planned orders. When the system planner confirms planned orders they become firm planned orders. After firm planned orders have been released they are scheduled receipts. Capacity requirements planning (CRP) uses the information from the associated routing file and related work center files to schedule production for planned orders, firm planned orders, and uncompleted portions of scheduled receipts (work in process). Once production is scheduled, the scheduled load and available capacity are compared. The planner uses the comparison information to tweak the scheduled production as necessary. Additional sources of manufacturing load include unplanned events like unexpected sales orders, special orders, scrap, and rework.

Source of Load in a Repetitive Manufacturing Environment

Repetitive manufacturing is manufacturing of one product or product family on a dedicated assembly line at a predetermined rate. This type of manufacturing is used in situations where a large volume of the product or product family is required. The master schedule sets the rate of manufacture, usually per hour or shift, rather than the required quantity and due date, so the manufacturing load comes from the required rate of production. In this environment, capacity requirements planning (CRP) is often unnecessary since available capacity does not have to be allocated among different product demands. Rough cut capacity planning can be used instead.

Effect of Unplanned Events on Manufacturing Load

Unplanned events that affect manufacturing load are product demands that were not forecast or planned for. These unplanned demands must be handled carefully in conjunction with the planned loading in order to maintain customer service. Unplanned events include extra sales orders, rework orders, special orders, and machine breakdowns. Extra sales orders are customer orders received that exceed the planned production quantity, or even customer orders for products not scheduled for production. Rework orders also require manufacturing capacity and must be scheduled into the system although not originally included. Special orders are one-time runs performed unexpectedly for customers. Machine breakdowns are another unexpected source of load. Quick repairs and temporarily increased capacity can ease the need for full-blown rescheduling. The effects of unexpected loads in manufacturing must be considered carefully. It may be better to refuse them if possible, particularly extra sales orders and special orders, due to the overall effect on manufacturing and meeting the previously existing requirements.

Lead-Time Management

The amount of work in process is a function of the amount of work released into production and the manufacturing lead time, so the manufacturing lead time is a primary determinant of the amount of work in process. Although the set lead times used in material requirements planning (MRP) may seem rigid, they are actually flexible. Priority jobs can be rushed through manufacturing, and work takes longer to complete when a work center is heavily loaded than when it is lightly loaded. Prioritizing production generally involves switching around inter-operational times (queue, wait, and move times) in order to accomplish certain goals. Actual manufacturing time is not changed. Effective lead-time management often involves focusing on inter-operational time. Principles of just-in time (JIT) manufacturing involve minimizing lead time by shortening queue time through decreasing batch sizes and set-up times. The same operation time will be needed to produce the same quantity of products, but producing smaller batches of products more often decreases the long waits for large batches to be processed.

Decreasing Manufacturing Lead Time

Work cells, groups of work centers arranged into production lines for particular products or product groups, decrease manufacturing lead time by shortening move time and queue time. When the work centers necessary for manufacturing the product are grouped together, work in process is fed directly from one work center to the following adjacent work center. This eliminates moving and queuing except at the initial input into the work cell.

When using JIT, operation set-up times are minimized. Long set-up times increase manufacturing lead time directly and indirectly. The longer the set-up time, the larger the batch size to compensate for the production capacity lost while setting up the manufacturing run. The large batch sizes used when set-up time is long increase the move time and queue time. If set-up time can be cut in half, batch size can be cut in half as well, and the number of manufacturing runs doubled. The same quantity can be produced with significantly reduced queue and wait times due to the smaller batch sizes.

Move and Queue Time

Both move time and queue time are components of the manufacturing lead time. The move time is the time spent transporting work in process between manufacturing operations. Move time varies greatly between companies. It can be short enough to be practically nonexistent or long enough to add several days to the manufacturing lead time. Move time does not affect production capacity. Queue time is the time that work in process spends at a work center before the set-up for its operation is begun. Queue time depends on the work center's capacity and current loading. Queue time typically comprises a large portion of the manufacturing lead time, and does not affect production capacity.

Set-up and Run Time

Both set-up time and run time are components of the manufacturing lead time. Planned set-up time is the theoretical length of time determined by industrial engineering for setting up a manufacturing run, while actual set-up time is the amount of time it actually takes to set up the manufacturing run. Set-up time not only adds to the manufacturing lead time but also consumes capacity, so it should be minimized. Unit run time is the time necessary for the actual processing of an item through a work center, and is multiplied by the lot size to determine the lot run time. Run time consumes capacity and adds to the manufacturing lead time.

Backlog

Backlog, orders that have been received and accepted but not yet filled, functions as a component of demand for manufactured goods. It is different from forecast demand in that it is real and not predicted. Backlog adds to the product demand, creating manufacturing load. In manufacturing, backlog can be a good thing since it represents actual future sales and not just projected sales. At the same time, backlog can be a bad thing in manufacturing because customer satisfaction may not be high with backlog customers because of the wait for goods, and this can result in less business later.

Intermittent Production and Project Manufacture

Intermittent production, or job shop production, is the production process flow in which similar work centers are grouped together within the manufacturing facility, and products are routed to the appropriate work centers. Each batch has its own specific routing. Intermittent production works best in facilities that produce small volumes of a large variety of products. The disadvantage of intermittent production is long inter-operational times. As jobs come into a work center, they queue. After processing is performed, they wait and then are moved. In an intermittent production environment, required capacity can be calculated and scheduled, but in practice long queues cause missed due dates.

Project manufacture is the production process flow used for manufacturing major structures like capital equipment and bridges. Lead time includes design, purchasing, manufacturing, and often installation. Project manufacture is controlled by dedicated project teams using tools such as Gantt charts and critical path diagrams.

FACTORS IMPACTING CAPACITY

FLOW MANUFACTURING, FLOW LINE MANUFACTURING, CELLULAR MANUFACTURING

In flow manufacturing, there is a steady, continuous flow of materials through production. Equipment is arranged according to the product processing, and not organized by function. Scheduling is determined by a set production rate. Flow lines and work cells are both types of flow manufacturing. Flow line manufacturing is a group of sequential workstations through which the same products or products requiring the same sequence of operations proceed one at a time. Scheduling is based on a set production rate and routings are not usually necessary. In cellular manufacturing, workstations are organized into work cells for producing specific parts. In all flow manufacturing, products are manufactured down a line or through a process, minimizing inter-operational time. The master schedule is used to plan capacity, and lower queue times help ensure that due dates are met.

REWORK, SCRAP, AND QUALITY

The amount of materials scrapped and/or reworked is a factor of the quality. High scrap and rework levels indicate low quality, which is expensive in manufacturing. When materials are scrapped, replacements must be manufactured, and rework materials go through manufacturing again. In both cases, the manufacturing load and thus capacity consumed are increased as a result of the poor quality. The scrap and rework percentages used for scheduling materials should also be applied to scheduling capacity. It is important for companies to maintain good quality in their production in order to minimize the lost capacity resulting from scrap and rework. In the past it was thought that improving quality was too expensive, but today it is understood that failing to improve quality is too expensive.

DETAILED CAPACITY PLANNING

THREE LEVELS OF MANUFACTURING PLANNING AND CONTROL

When considering detailed capacity planning, it is important to do so within the framework of the manufacturing planning and control system. The manufacturing planning and control system includes three descending levels: top management planning, operations management planning and operations management execution. Top management planning entails business planning and sales and operation planning. Operations management planning entails using the business and operation plans from top management to develop the master production schedule (MPS) and the material requirements plan. Operations management execution entails applying and implementing the MPS and material requirements plan in low-level manufacturing, through executing the daily schedule by controlling the volume of work and production priority sequence.

- Techniques used at the top management level: In top management planning, *the* detailed capacity planning technique employed is resource requirements planning. Resource requirements planning is used to verify the viability of the sales and operation plan, to make sure the plan can be executed with the available resources. If the plan is not checked initially, frustration and failure can result from trying to do something that is not possible. If the resource requirements planning indicates that the plan is not feasible with the available resources, either the resource availability or the sales and operation plan must be changed.
- Techniques used at the operations management planning: In operations planning, the detailed capacity planning techniques employed are rough cut capacity planning (RCCP) and capacity requirements planning (CRP). RCCP is used to check the master production schedule for feasibility, and CRP us used to check the material requirements plan for feasibility. Without performing RCCP and CRP and adjusting scheduling accordingly, manufacturing would have an uneven workload, possibly resulting in missed deadlines in manufacturing and ultimately in filling customer orders.
- Techniques used in operations management execution: The detailed capacity planning techniques employed are input/output control and dispatching. Input/output control is used to regulate the volume of work released into manufacturing in order to maintain scheduled output. Dispatching is used to prioritize and sequence production tasks in order to maintain scheduled output.

Rough Cut Capacity Planning

RCCP is a simulation and modeling technique used in detailed capacity planning to verify that the master production schedule (MPS) developed from the sales and operation plan is feasible by comparing MPS resource requirements to the availability of critical resources such as personnel, equipment, inventory storage space, capability and sometimes money by time period and indicating any potential over- and under-capacity situations. When the master scheduler in operations management planning receives the sales and operation plan (usually in months) from top management planning and from it develops an MPS (usually in weeks or days), the manufacturing load may be uneven. RCCP roughly indicates imbalances, which the scheduler uses to adjust the MPS appropriately to even out manufacturing load. The MPS is then released for use in material requirements planning (MRP).

Compared to CRP

As the name implies, RCCP is rough. It is an overall comparison of master production schedule (MPS) requirements to the availability of key resources. From RCCP it is determined whether the overall goals are feasible, or if they need to be adjusted. It is not until after RCCP is performed that the overall goals are broken down into the lower level goals. The MPS requirements (overall goals) are broken down into the material plan (specific goals) through the material requirements planning (MRP) process. MRP is in turn used to perform CRP, through which the feasibility of the material plan is verified. MRP and CRP are both detailed and specific, encompassing all individual materials and operations required for production. While RCCP reconciles the overall production requirements with the overall production capacity, CRP reconciles the production requirements and production capacity for each individual operation and material.

INPUT/OUTPUT CONTROL

Input/output control, a tool for controlling production capacity in which both the planned and actual manufacturing inputs and outputs of individual work centers are monitored and compared, is used to control the volume of work released into manufacturing. The planned inputs and outputs are generated by capacity requirements planning (CRP). Comparing the planned inputs to the actual inputs indicates if the work center is receiving the input necessary to achieve planned output. If it is not, there is a problem in the feeder work center. Comparing the planned outputs to the actual outputs indicates if the work center is meeting production goals. If the feeder work center is supplying the planned input, the work center should meet production goals. If it does not, there is a problem within the work center itself. The planner uses this information to make necessary adjustments to meet the production plan. Input/output control is also called production monitoring.

OPERATIONS MANAGEMENT PLANNING

In operations management planning, the master production schedule (MPS) which has been verified by rough cut capacity planning serves as the input to material requirements planning (MRP), through which is generated the material plan, or future manufacturing orders. Through CRP, the material plan, specifically the individual manufacturing orders, are broken down into the individual operations required using the product routing data. Each operation is broken down into standard hours required for production of materials, resulting in figures for hours required per work center per time period. This information is compared to the work center availability, and the planner uses the comparison data to provide a balanced load to each work center. If manufacturing load is imbalanced, manufacturing due dates and ultimately customer order deadlines may not be met. Additionally, manufacturing may lose trust in planning and ignore imbalanced schedules.

SCHEDULING MANUFACTURING OPERATIONS

After material requirements planning (MRP) is performed, capacity requirements planning (CRP) is performed and reconciled to the material plan and manufacturing operations are scheduled. For effective manufacturing, the production schedule must provide balanced loading, and, if desired, level loading because load leveling occurs at the production plan level. If level loading is not chosen, then chase scheduling is used. At lower levels of manufacturing, level scheduling is performed through either mixed model production or rate-based scheduling, depending on the production environment. Additional scheduling frameworks that can be chosen include synchronous manufacturing and bottleneck scheduling. In all of these scheduling techniques, the work required in standard hours is determined and planned. The planner is responsible for doing any manual work necessary such as rescheduling or handling capacity problems so that the schedule is feasible and the manufacturing demand can be met.

MANUFACTURING LOAD LEVELING

Load leveling is a process used to provide level loading to manufacturing. Level production plans produce level master production schedules (MPS), but this does not necessarily lead to level loading in the lower levels of production. Manufacturing orders are planned through material requirements planning (MRP) based on the MPS, but since lead times and operations required vary the resulting lower level loading may not be level. The lower levels of manufacturing are planned using backward or forward loading in conjunction with infinite or finite scheduling. Although load leveling provides the advantage of a level manufacturing workload, it can also result in high product inventory levels prior to periods of high demand, which can be a disadvantage.

Scheduling of Logistics Operations

Logistics refers to all aspects of planning and executing the material flow, including ordering, purchasing, transporting, and handling materials. Once production schedules have been established, material order dates can be confirmed and acted upon. Later changes that develop will generate action messages within the material requirements planning (MRP) system to inform the planner and the buyer so they can take appropriate action such as renegotiating delivery dates, which in turn are updated in the plan. Logistics operations are scheduled and rescheduled in order to line up the scheduled receipts with the material requirements, to balance demand with supply.

Manufacturing Plan Timing

Manufacturing should be planned far enough in advance that critical resource capability can be increased as necessary to meet forecast demand changes. The four critical manufacturing resources are personnel, facilities, machinery, and finances. Increasing personnel entails hiring and training new workers. Training time varies from industry to industry, and in more specialized industries can be quite lengthy. Time required for adding manufacturing equipment also varies considerably. Time required can be short if standard equipment is purchased from vendors, but time required can be considerable if custom-built capital equipment is used. Adding manufacturing facilities is an involved process. The need for the facility must be justified, and the facility must be approved by top management and constructed. Finances are required when major capacity increases are undertaken, and freeing up finances within a company is a time-consuming process. The most common method of freeing up assets is through inventory reduction. A company's future planning should extend to the time necessary to perform the lengthiest of these capacity-increasing processes.

Planning Horizon

As is the case in material requirements planning (MRP), capacity requirements planning (CRP) uses the planning horizon set by the master production schedule (MPS). The time fence set in the MPS is the length of time necessary for assembling products and purchasing and manufacturing parts and components for products (cumulative lead time) and a look ahead period for planning future purchases based on the applicable ordering policies in time to meet future demand (batching period). Since overall manufacturing requirements and capability are checked through resource requirements planning at the production plan level and loading and availability of critical resources are checked through rough cut capacity planning at the master schedule level, the MPS planning horizon generally provides enough time for load and capacity balancing of individual work centers and operations. If the MPS planning horizon is for some reason shorter than the cumulative lead time plus a batching period, then there will be insufficient time for planning production, purchasing supplies, and assembling goods according to the individual planned lead times.

Queuing

The queue for a manufacturing work center or operation is the line of work orders waiting to be processed. Although the work canter capacity may be sufficient for the average load for the time period, the random timing of arrivals within the time period may cause a queue at specific times when the arrival rate exceeds the operation's processing rate. This occurs because the arrival time of work orders is random and not specifically planned. As time progresses, the operation should catch back up with the work order flow since the overall capacity meets the average loading. In the meantime, however, some work orders have been delayed.

Excessive queuing, which can be caused by the random arrival of work orders at a work station even if the average load for the time period is balanced by available production capacity at the work center in question, causes manufacturing delays. The process lead time for the work orders increases as the queue length increases. If the backup of work orders is severe enough, the queue may have to be examined and a large job rescheduled or rerouted so that other jobs can continue on time. The priority system determines how queuing is handled by setting the sequencing rules by which the queue will be processed. Priority system sequencing rules can be based on scheduled start date, scheduled completion date, queue ratio, processing time required, or order of arrival in the queue (first in first out). The priority system is executed by means of a daily dispatch list at each work center detailing current priorities and work sequence.

Manufacturing Loading Techniques

Manufacturing can be loaded according to an infinite or a finite loading scheme in conjunction with backward, forward, or central point scheduling. In all infinite loading, there is potential for overloading since available capacity is not considered because it is assumed to be infinite. Overloading can causes delays and can ultimately cause missed completion dates if not handled appropriately by the system scheduler and manufacturing. Finite loading takes available capacity into account, through add-on scheduling facilities like advanced planning and scheduling (APS). In both finite and infinite loading, it is necessary to consider discrepancies between the actual manufacturing lead times and the system's defined lead times, since inconsistencies between the two can also lead to delays and missed completion dates if not handled well.

Infinite Loading

Infinite loading is the default framework for loading manufacturing in most material requirements planning (MRP) and capacity requirements planning (CRP) systems. When forward scheduling is used with infinite loading, processing begins at the planned start date and ends at the time determined from the start date by system lead times; thus, forward scheduled infinite loading order releases occur at the start date planned in the master schedule. Backward scheduled infinite loading is based on the required completion date, and the appropriate lead times are subtracted from the end date to determine the start date, so orders are released into manufacturing on the start date calculated through the backward scheduled infinite loading process. Similarly, in central point scheduled infinite loading the orders are released into manufacturing on the date backward scheduled from the central point.

Advanced Planning and Scheduling

Advanced planning and scheduling (APS) is defined as techniques for simulation and optimization using advanced mathematical algorithms and/or logic in order to analyze and plan manufacturing materials and capacity simultaneously rather than in isolation for the near and distant future. APS systems incorporate a wide range of constraints, rules, and priorities into their calculations, and consist of the five main components demand planning, production planning, production scheduling, distribution planning and transportation planning. APS is used in finite loading capacity scheduling to plan multiple operations per work center per day by calculating exact start and stop times using queuing and priority data. This is an improvement over the typical daily scheduling of manufacturing and capacity requirements planning (MRP and CRP) that leave overload situations to be handled by human ingenuity alone.

Capacity Management

Capacity management is the oversight of production capability, including identifying that capability and adjusting it as necessary, in order to fulfill manufacturing requirements set forth by the master schedule, master production schedule, material requirements plan and the dispatch list. Capacity management is performed at different levels, just as production requirements are set at different levels. The four levels of capacity management are resource requirements planning, rough cut capacity planning, capacity requirements planning and input/output control. Through capacity management, the capacity itself and/or the corresponding load placed on the capacity is/are adjusted to meet manufacturing requirements. Safety capacity and tooling requirements scheduling can also be used. Safety capacity balances unplanned work, and is helpful in production environments with unpredictable load variability. Scheduling tooling requirements is necessary in production environments where specialized tooling not associated with work centers is used. Effective and efficient capacity management is necessary for successful operations planning and control.

Safety Capacity

Safety capacity is a portion of production capability that is not utilized in order to provide extra available capacity in case of planned down time like preventive maintenance, unplanned down time like equipment breakdowns, and unscheduled work like scrap and rework. Productive capacity, safety capacity and excess capacity together comprise the total capacity. In a job shop production environment, scheduling an operation for more than 80% of its production capacity results in increased work in process, and thus longer queuing and lead times. Either the capacity must be increased or the customer service level will decrease. Safety capacity can be implemented by capping the percentage of available capacity that can be scheduled for manufacturing jobs or by planting an artificial product and routing in the master production schedule (MPS).

Maintenance

Maintenance is an important consideration in capacity management, since time spent on maintenance is nonproductive time for the piece of equipment, and perhaps the entire work cell, in question. Nonproductive time can lead to production delays and missed completion dates. Breakdown maintenance is particularly disruptive to production since it occurs unexpectedly, interrupting and delaying production. Breakdown maintenance also leads to less reliable equipment. Planned maintenance is superior to breakdown maintenance since the machines are kept in better working order and downtime is usually scheduled. Planned maintenance can be accounted for in the production planning, and may even occur at production down times like nights, weekends and holidays so that available capacity is unchanged. Maintenance is especially important in work cell based manufacturing, since downtime for one machine equates to downtime for the entire work cell.

Accessory Equipment

Accessory equipment such as tooling and gauges is an important consideration in capacity management because it can delay manufacturing when the equipment is necessary but unavailable. Since accessory equipment is not associated with or dedicated to a particular work center, it is not necessarily available when a job requiring it arrives at a work center for processing. It could be in use elsewhere at the time. Tooling is used for the actual processing of goods through an operation, so tool set-up time and tool life as well as availability must be considered in scheduling.

Output of Capacity Planning

The output of capacity planning is information, specifically the comparison data between manufacturing loading and production capacity at every level of manufacturing at all times for which manufacturing is planned. The information is typically presented as a percentage load report or a load versus capacity summary report for a specified time period into the future including any past due work. Capacity planning does not solve load and capacity imbalances but rather points them out. It is the responsibility of the system planner to resolve the imbalances manually in conjunction with manufacturing. Tools available for this purpose include input/output control, operations sequencing, overtime, subcontracting, alternate routing, rescheduling, and order splitting.

BALANCING LOAD AND CAPACITY

SYSTEM PLANNER

The system planner uses the input/output control report to understand what is going on in manufacturing, in particular how the planned and actual inputs and outputs are lining up and any cumulative variances that are building up. The planner then uses this information to adjust the release of work orders into manufacturing. Only work that can be accomplished should be released into manufacturing, so releases should slow down and be limited to the most urgent jobs when backlogs accrue. The planner must work with manufacturing to alleviate the backlog, perhaps through overtime or even rescheduling jobs. One practical measure that can be taken is setting limits on the allowable amount of work in process. Once the work in process exceeds the limit, action must be taken. Another practical measure is rescheduling jobs that have not yet started rather than trying to change what is happening with work in process since this can be logistically difficult.

OPERATIONS SEQUENCING

Operations sequencing is the process of establishing low-level manufacturing priorities within the production environment through prioritizing and sequencing the work to be performed. The system planner uses the capacity planning output information and the known manufacturing priorities to perform operations sequencing. The system planner then formulates a daily dispatch list to communicate to manufacturing the specific priorities and work sequencing to follow to meet production goals and deadlines. The daily dispatch list is broken down per work center or cell, and should be developed in conjunction with manufacturing so that it is practical and will be followed.

OVERTIME

Overtime is the practice of assigning extra work hours to operations personnel. Overtime is a tool that manufacturing supervision uses in response to daily dispatch lists and percentage load reports to resolve overload situations or to fulfill urgent priorities. It is a quick and easy way to increase production capacity to meet loading that is over capacity. When using overtime, it is important to remember that worker performance decreases with the length of time worked, so this tool is best used infrequently and in moderation.

RESCHEDULING

Rescheduling is the practice of changing the production schedule in response to overload situations or other obstacles. The planner can reschedule required work to fit into the available capacity by moving jobs from the originally scheduled, overloaded time period, to an earlier or later under-loaded time period. The planner must consider promised customer delivery dates as well as the effect on other work centers as he contemplates rescheduling manufacturing.

SUBCONTRACTING

Subcontracting is the practice of paying an external worker or company for manufacturing work. Subcontractors are paid by time or volume, and are not considered personnel. Subcontracting can be used effectively to perform work involving highly specialized labor and/or equipment, to lower the cost of routine work which does not involve special skill or equipment, or to meet capacity requirements in overload situations, especially if the factory is generally overloaded. Subcontracting is a long-term, planned solution since it takes time to locate and evaluate appropriate providers and develop partnerships with them. The system planner or planning department typically utilizes subcontracting in response to the master production schedule (MPS) and rough-cut capacity planning (RCCP) or manufacturing and capacity requirements planning (MRP and CRP).

Alternate Routing

Alternate routing is the practice of using secondary production routings for items slated to pass through an overloaded work center or cell. Even though production planning with resource requirements planning and the rough-cut-capacity-planned master production schedule (MPS) may produce balanced overall production goals, this balance does not necessarily trickle down to individual work centers. When work centers are overloaded, alternate routings can be used to meet the production schedule. Approved alternate routings are maintained as an information field in the product routing sheets, or as a secondary routing. Planning systems use the default or primary routing, so using alternate routings for production is a manual decision made by the planner to resolve immediate and near-future overloading situations.

Order Splitting

Order splitting is the practice of dividing a production lot into two parts in order to get one portion of the lot through manufacturing quickly to meet a specific priority. The first, usually smaller, portion of the batch is expedited through production, while the second proceeds as planned. If the decision is made to split the order before it has been released into manufacturing, the planner may release a small order to be expedited, and then release a regularly sized order at the scheduled time instead of splitting a regularly sized order. Otherwise, the batch is simply divided. The smaller, expedited order runs in less time and consumes less capacity because it is smaller in size, but the cost of a second operation set-up is incurred.

Capacity Planning Performance Measurements

Ratio of Planned Workload to Available Capacity

The system planner uses capacity requirements planning (CRP) to understand the planned workload and detect any imbalances. He uses information about projected imbalances to make appropriate corrections. One way to measure success of CRP is to compare planned workload to available capacity. This ratio indicates how well the system planner has used CRP to load manufacturing at or below capacity. If the workload is much greater than the capacity, either too much work was scheduled in the master production schedule (MPS) or variation in low-level lead times caused imbalances even though the overall workload and capacity were balanced. If too much work is required by the MPS, overloads, missed completion dates, and rescheduling will result. Increasing capacity or rescheduling into the future are the only solutions. If low-level lead-time variation causes imbalances, the planner's skill to rebalance the lower level load and capacity is essential for finding a solution. Improving the planned workload to available capacity results in higher productivity and reduced idle time and overtime.

Past Due Load

The past due load is work assigned to manufacturing which is still incomplete at its due date, indicating failure of the detailed capacity planning process for those jobs that are past due. There are many possible causes for missed completion dates, including master production schedule (MPS) overload, extremely imbalanced loading, material and personnel shortages, disregarding the daily dispatch list, and equipment malfunctions. Not all of these situations are under the planner's control, but the planner must still respond to them to avoid past due work. Ideally, the planner uses the capacity requirements planning (CRP) data to reorganize production as necessary and responds to unplanned circumstances appropriately to avoid past due work. Once there is past due work, the planner must take action to complete that job as well as other work in process without incurring additional past due load.

Work in Process (WIP)

The amount of manufacturing WIP serves as a useful detailed capacity planning performance measurement. The level of WIP is a reflection of discrepancies between planned and actual lead times and the resulting amount of manufacturing queuing, which in turn reflect the effectiveness of the work management and material flow through manufacturing. WIP serves as a performance measurement in two ways, through comparison to a target WIP level and through tracking improvement by monitoring changes in WIP over time. A rough, target WIP level can be calculated simply by multiplying the average manufacturing lead time by the materials released into manufacturing per time period. The accuracy of the target depends on the accuracy of the lead-time figure. WIP can also be monitored through successive time periods to determine if the detailed capacity planning and execution is getting better or worse.

Planned Lead Time

Planned lead time is an important factor in detailed capacity planning performance. The accuracy of the planned lead time itself is a key factor in timely manufacturing, both in meeting scheduled goals and in improving manufacturing performance over time. If the planned lead time is shorter than actually required, then the manufacturing process takes longer than necessary since actual lead times tend to be as long as planned lead times whether the full planned lead time is required or not. Conversely, if the planned lead time is too short, then the schedule is unrealistic and scheduled goals are missed. Continually improving lead times and reflecting those improvements in the planning are keys to improving detailed capacity planning and manufacturing performance.

Capacity Planning System Interaction

Capacity planning does not occur in isolation, but in relationship with other planning and control subsystems in the manufacturing environment. The business and operations planning processes in top management planning produce the master schedule, from which is developed the master production schedule (MPS). The MPS drives the material planning process, which produces the material plan. The material plan is verified for production viability through capacity planning. Capacity planning serves as a feedback loop to material planning as well as a mechanism for scheduling production. Through capacity planning the material requirements are broken down into the individual operations necessary for production and the capacity required. The required production capacity is then compared to the available capacity to determine the manufacturing schedule per work center per time period, and changes can be made to the material plan if necessary.

Top Management Planning

Top management planning entails business planning and sales and operation planning. It is at this level that the forecast finished goods demand is set and/or actual customer orders are considered to develop a master schedule. Operations management planning uses the master schedule to set the master production schedule (MPS), which specifies finished goods requirements by quantity and date. The MPS drives the material planning process, and the capacity planning process verifies that production capacity is available to meet the material plan and sets the production schedule. Business planning sets the overall demand for which the capacity planning process verifies capacity availability and schedules production. The two processes working together close the demand and supply loop between master planning and final assembly and configuration of finished goods.

Internal Interactions

Within detailed operations planning, the required supply of internally manufactured materials is reconciled with the production capability in order to provide the required materials in the required quantities by the required time. Capacity requirements planning (CRP) first uses the routing information for required items to break down the material requirements into individual operations and determine their run times, establishing the production capacity required and allowing scheduling of operations. If the required workload cannot be balanced, the capacity must be increased or the material plan, master productions schedule (MPS), master schedule, etc., may have to be reviewed and changed accordingly.

Between Capacity Planning and Manufacturing Execution and Control

The interaction between capacity planning and manufacturing execution and control reconciles the scheduled use of production capacity with the actual production so that the production goals and schedule are met. Material requirements planning (MRP) provides a detailed material plan, from which capacity requirements planning (CRP) or other operations scheduling modules determine the individual operations and required capacity per time period. A dispatch list is then produced daily for each manufacturing work center to follow. Keeping the system information updated keeps the daily dispatch list up-to-date and manufacturing functioning according to current goals and schedules. Short-range capacity execution is carried out through input/output control, in which schedule inputs and outputs are monitored per work center to adjust the input if necessary.

Base Series and Critical Ratio

Base series is a tool for forecasting product demand in seasonal industries; the base series is a set of factors indicating the demand over time in a seasonal cycle, usually based on past demand; the average of the factors in the series is one, and factors greater than one indicate higher than average demand for the corresponding time period, while factors less than one indicate less than average demand for the corresponding time period; a base series can also be called a base index or seasonal index

Critical ratio is a dispatching rule for prioritizing and sequencing jobs dispatched to manufacturing in which the ratio of time until the job's due date to the time necessary to complete the job is calculated; a critical ratio of one means that the job is exactly on schedule, a critical ratio above one means that the job is ahead of schedule, and a critical ratio below one means that the job is behind schedule

Important Terms

Byproduct: A product of value that is produced inadvertently through the production of a different demanded product; byproducts are not scheduled for production, but as receipts that are inventoried following the production process.

Effectivity date: The scheduled time when changes to bills of material, operation routings, or other details related to product manufacture take effect; the effectivity date is important information for material and production planning so that manufacturing flow is not interrupted by the changes.

Flexibility: The ability to respond well and quickly to changing customer demand and requests; customer response.

Gateway work center: The first operation or process in a product's routing

Idle capacity: Production capability that remains unused either inadvertently due to lack of demand or purposefully as a safety net to meet unanticipated demand.

Idle time: The time in which a manufacturing operation is not actively used for production either inadvertently due to lack of demand or available materials or purposefully for setup and maintenance purposes.

Load profile: A report detailing the planned and actual capacity requirements over time for a particular manufacturing resource either numerically or graphically; the load profile may break down the load into its various sources.

Machine center: A group of machines processing a common family of goods that comprises an individual work center and is treated as one unit for planning and routing purposes.

Machine hours: The actual amount of time in use recorded by a production machine and used to calculate efficiency and utilization.

Manufacturing order: An authorization for the manufacture of the number and types of parts specified; manufacturing orders can also be called job orders, manufacturing authorizations, production orders, production releases, run orders, shop orders, and work orders.

Manufacturing strategy: A policy in line with the overall business goals used within a particular production environment to prioritize and use manufacturing resources.

Production activity control (PAC): The process of managing manufacturing through routing and dispatching manufacturing work and controlling suppliers; PAC entails planning, managing, monitoring and improving manufacturing operations; PAC can also be called shop floor control.

Pull system: A method of filling demand triggered by the demand itself; as parts are required, they are produced to be used or taken from stock and used which triggers the replenishment of the stock; pull systems can be used in inventory, manufacturing, and distribution.

Push system: A method of filling demand in which central planning and scheduling forecast demand and trigger production and acquisition of parts; push systems can be used in inventory, manufacturing, and distribution.

Quality: The degree to which goods or services meet requirements and are usable; negatively, quality is the absence of deviations from specifications, and positively, quality is the degree of customer satisfaction resulting from the product.

Total quality management (TQM): A holistic, formalized approach to business success through customer satisfaction that involves all workers at every level in improving every aspect of the business; TQM is based on Japanese-style quality management.

Total productive maintenance (TPM): A holistic, formalized approach to preventive maintenance and continual process improvement in which machine operators and all other qualified personnel participate in increasing process flexibility, decreasing material handling, and promoting continuous manufacturing flow.

Zero inventory: The target level of stock to be maintained in a just-in-time production environment, where inventory is not considered an asset but rather a liability.

Capacity Terms

Capacity: The maximum production capability in output per time period of a particular factory, process, work center, machine, or worker.

Load: The amount of work actually assigned or released to a particular factory, process, work center, machine or worker during a given time period; load is usually measured in standard work hours and sometimes measured in production units.

CRP horizon: The length of time into the future for which the capacity requirements are planned, set by the master production schedule (MPS); practically, the time covered by CRP reports should be set by the purpose for which the report is generated: a report generated for use in long-term planning should include the whole CRP horizon, while a report for planning manufacturing overtime for the upcoming week should cover that week.

Manufacturing Terms

Make-to-order company: A company that manufactures products in response to actual customer orders, rather than in response to forecast demand.

Make-to-stock company: A company that manufactures standard products in response to the forecast demand for those products, stores them in inventory, and sells them as they are when customers order them; manufacturing and material ordering requirements are set by forecast product demand, and finished goods go to replenish the finished goods store.

Mixed manufacturing company: A company in which products are made-to-order as well as made-to-stock; make-to-order production and make-to-stock production are mixed to balance the manufacturing load by prioritizing make-to-order production and allocating remaining production capacity to make-to-stock production.

Job shop: A production environment in which equipment in a factory is organized into groups by function and batches of goods follow a production routing from group to group through the facility for processing; the equipment is used for general purposes, and many different products can be produced and/or specialized in the facility based on their individual routing; capacity requirements planning (CRP) is a key tool for managing job shop operations; job shop manufacture is also called intermittent production.

Repetitive manufacture: A production environment in which discrete products or product families are repeatedly manufactured in large volumes on dedicated assembly lines according to rate-based schedules rather than orders, with little or no production variation.

Process manufacture: A production environment in which gases, liquids, and/or powders are processed by mixing, separating, forming, and/or performing chemical reactions, characterized by low product complexity, little or no product variation, and dedicated manufacturing facilities.

Process, Order, and Constraint Oriented Loading

Process-oriented finite loading is a finite loading technique in which manufacturing throughput is maximized by minimizing individual operation delays, ultimately minimizing order delays; process-oriented finite loading is performed by loading work required by an order or a group of orders into a process or work center according to operation and, to a lesser degree, order priorities as limited by the available capacity.

Order-oriented finite loading is a finite loading technique in which capacity utilization is maximized or the number of orders executed and/or percentage of orders delivered on time is maximized; order-oriented finite loading is performed by loading and scheduling manufacturing according to order priorities as limited by available capacity.

Constraint-oriented finite loading is a finite loading technique in which manufacturing throughput is maximized by planning around the constraints of bottleneck work centers; operations downstream from the bottleneck are scheduled forward in large lot sizes, while upstream operations are scheduled backwards from the bottleneck in small lot sizes; at the constraint, the small lots are joined into large lots for further processing.

Central Point Scheduling, Slack Time and Probable Scheduling

Central point scheduling: Capacity and load balancing and scheduling technique in which scheduling is centered around a critical process or manufacturing bottleneck; the scheduling of the critical process is slated first according to available capacity, with prior processes backward scheduled from the critical point and later processes forward scheduled from the critical point.

Slack time: The difference between the scheduled completion date and the actual projected completion date calculated once processing has begun based on the progress.

Probable scheduling: A new capacity and load balancing technique in which operations are rescheduled as manufacturing occurs based on the slack time; manufacturing lead times can be shortened or lengthened as indicated by the slack time, resulting in new probable process start and end times.

Scheduling Manufacturing Operations Terms

Load leveling: A technique for obtaining manufacturing labor and/or material loading that is feasible and evenly distributed over time by spacing manufacturing orders, rescheduling operations, or otherwise rearranging demand; load leveling is also called capacity smoothing and level loading.

Chase scheduling: A technique for manufacturing loading and scheduling in which loading and scheduling vary with the demand; chase scheduling is the opposite of load leveling.

Level scheduling: The practice of providing a constant, consistent and balanced production workload.

Mixed model production: A production environment characterized by flexibility, short lead times, and small batches in which a variety of products are produced per time period, usually daily, in the quantity demanded in that same time period, rather than producing and stocking large batches of each item.

Rate-based scheduling: A production scheduling technique used in repetitive manufacture in which scheduling is based on a time period's production rate specified by the master production schedule (MPS) and not on manufacturing orders or demand.

Synchronous manufacturing: A production environment in which the entire manufacturing flow is orchestrated to meet demand through linking together material supply, levels of manufacturing and demand and eliminating work in process and interim inventories; in synchronous manufacturing even and balanced loading of demand is required, and each process step feeds into the next process step in the quantity and timing required to meet demand.

Bottleneck scheduling: Scheduling of manufacturing centered on the constraining work center; the constraining work center is scheduled first, and then the rest of manufacturing is backward and forward scheduled from that critical point; bottleneck scheduling is also called central point scheduling.

MAINTENANCE TERMS

Planned maintenance: A method for maintaining production equipment in which machine downtimes are scheduled for preventive maintenance and service, set either by the maintenance department and worked around by manufacturing or set by manufacturing with the cooperation of the maintenance department.

Breakdown maintenance: A method, or the lack thereof, for maintaining production equipment in which the machines are operated until they malfunction, at which point the maintenance department makes necessary repairs.

Accessory equipment: Equipment used in manufacturing that is not associated with or dedicated to a particular work center, such as tools and gauges.

Tooling: Accessory equipment used for processing particular goods, usually specified in the routing, that is not typically a part of the operation performed by the work center; the same tool can be used in multiple work centers.

Gauge: An accessory tool used by process personnel or inspectors to verify that the goods processed fall within specifications.

Planning Procurement and External Sources of Supply

Process

Procurement is the purchasing of goods and materials required for manufacturing and any other tasks associated with the purchasing process, including finding, rating, and selecting suppliers as well as communicating requirements to, building relationships with, and negotiating contracts with suppliers. Traditionally, manufacturers have had adversarial relationships with their suppliers, but the relationships between manufacturers and their suppliers are now becoming long-term partnerships, where the two work together to meet the manufacturer's production goals. The quality, delivery performance, and responsiveness of the supplier are key characteristics considered when forming these partnerships.

Supplier Partnerships

A supplier partnership is a relationship between a supplier and their customer in which the two companies work together as one entity to meet the customer's goals. This teamwork to accomplish the goal can provide a competitive advantage and continuous improvement when done well. This relationship usually develops in situations where the supplier has a skill or service that the customer needs but does not have and the partnership would be advantageous to both companies. Supplier partnerships are good for the supplier because they guarantee and even increase the customer's business with that supplier. Supplier partnerships are good for the manufacturer because of convenience and consistency. High-quality parts are delivered on time to the point of use, providing significant savings. Through supplier partnerships, suppliers and their customers collaborate even on research and development.

Three Types of Supplier Partnerships

- Strategic alliance: Supplier partnership on the overall business level in which a supplier and their customer agree to work together to streamline their operations by eliminating duplication between them; costs are reduced while maintaining customer service, resulting in a competitive advantage.
- Technical and commercial partnering: Supplier partnership on the product level in which a supplier and their customer work together to develop a particular product; the supplier develops and manufactures a product for the customer to use in manufacturing; the supplier and customer share the development costs.
- Operational partnering: Supplier partnership on the part level in which a supplier agrees to provide standard parts for their customer to use in manufacturing.

Supplier-Customer Relationships

In the current manufacturing environment, relationships between suppliers and their customers are progressing from adversarial and non-committal to trusting, cooperative and long-term. These relationships are characterized by open communication, sharing of information and partnership to meet common goals. In this environment, customers focus on building relationships with fewer suppliers, and choose them based on quality, timeliness, and responsiveness rather than cost alone. The customer typically requires the supplier to pass a rigorous initial or even annual selection and negotiation process, the customer clearly communicates reliable requirements to the supplier, the customer pays bills on schedule and visits are made back and forth so the customer can perform quality audits of the supplier and the supplier can understand the customer's requirements.

Customers and Suppliers Interaction

Customer and supplier integration is the joining of the two companies to work together as partners, based on the idea that the supplier prospers as their buyer prospers. The supplier and buyer working together can reduce costs more and produce a better finished product than the two could produce working independently. Integration requires a long-term working relationship between the parties. The supplier is involved in the buyer's design process, long-term contracts enable the supplier to more effectively and efficiently plan material and manufacturing, and the supplier engages in continuous quality improvement including tools like statistical process control. The supplier can ultimately become a certified supplier, in which case incoming inspection of their goods is no longer necessary.

Single and Multiple Sourcing

Multiple sourcing is the use of more than one supplier to provide a required material. Traditionally, multiple sourcing has been used in manufacturing to guarantee continuous part availability, but variation between suppliers can be a problem. Single sourcing is the use of only one supplier to provide a required material. In the current manufacturing environment, single sourcing is preferred. Although there is some risk in relying solely on one supplier for a part, the quality and reliability built through a single-source partner relationship is higher than through multiple sourcing. Single-source suppliers must demonstrate excellence and continual quality improvement evidenced by parts delivered.

Evaluation of Potential Partners and Certified Suppliers

As a company delves into supplier partnerships, they typically begin with their current suppliers. A questionnaire is sent to the suppliers to gauge potential partners. From the questionnaire results, potential suppliers are selected for site visits. The site visits include auditing the manufacturer's production, design, and business processes and facilities, as well as management interviews. The investigation of potential partners can also include references from other customers; the supplier's attitude, both in management and personnel, toward change, total quality management techniques, continuous improvement and customer satisfaction; the feasibility of partnership considering the supplier's location, technical expertise, equipment and manufacturing practices; and national and/or international registrations and/or certifications. Every company will also have individual concerns related to their industry and company.

Business Aspects to Be Considered Before Entering a Supplier Partnership

The business soundness of a potential partner is an important consideration for qualifying potential partners. Financial and business soundness is required to form a healthy partnership. Tests of financial soundness include the liquid ratio and examination of the internal costing system. The liquid ratio verifies that the company's liquid assets, which consist of available cash plus debts owed to the company, exceed their debts. The company's internal costing system is evaluated to determine if the internal costing is realistic. For the suppliers, important considerations before entering a partnership include the customer's timeliness in paying bills and their treatment of suppliers.

The existence of supplier partnerships does not guarantee that the customer's objectives are met through the relationship. The quality of the relationship itself must be developed and assessed. Continuous improvement is a required characteristic for a healthy partnership. After both companies sign the formal partnership agreement, the relationship must expand beyond management to encompass cooperation among personnel at all levels in both companies. Methods for procurement, introduction of new products, and engineering changes need to be agreed upon and executed accordingly. Open communication and appropriate training are also essential to the task of building trust and establishing a strong, healthy partnership.

The Procurement Steps That Must Be Agreed Upon in a Supplier Partnership

The first step in procurement is how the customer's demand for goods will be communicated to and fulfilled by the supplier. The customer may generate a material plan that is communicated to and fulfilled by the supplier, or the supplier may release product to the customer as the need arises through consignment stock, a kanban system or some other method. The mode(s) of communication between the supplier and customer must also be established. A designated customer service representative for the supplier and a designated buyer for the customer can handle all communication between the companies, or the company planners can communicate directly. The delivery of goods must also be agreed upon. In supplier partnerships, it is common for the supplier to be certified which means that deliveries can be made directly to the point of use, bypassing several material-handling stages. The final step in procurement is payment. Payment can be made per delivery, for deliveries made per time period, upon use, or upon production.

Introducing New Products into a Supplier Partnership

New products can be introduced in two ways. Either the customer is designing their end product or they already have specifications for the end product to be produced. In the first case, the supplier can be involved in the design process from the outset. This is called early purchasing involvement. The supplier provides specialized skills and information to the designers so that the end product will be built from parts that are easy for the supplier to make, benefiting both supplier and customer. When the customer already has the design for the product to be produced, the interaction between the customer and supplier is a bit different. In this situation the primary consideration is the supplier's ability to produce the required part(s). Timing can be an issue, since the supplier may have to buy equipment or tooling to manufacture the required part and the quality of its production must be established.

Making Engineering Changes Within the Context of Supplier Partnerships

Within the typical context of supplier partnerships in the current manufacturing environment, inventory levels are low, product designs are simplified, engineering changes are minimized since the design process is holistic and thorough, and necessary changes are quickly implemented. Although participative design minimizes changes, some changes can still be necessary. When changes are necessary, they must be organized and controlled. The bill of material, which is essentially a roadmap for manufacturing the product, must not change haphazardly. The three primary areas of engineering change organization and control are authorization, implementation, and communication of the change. The supplier is primarily involved with the communication area of engineering changes, since learning of required changes to the goods they supply is critical.

Supplier Certification

Supplier certification is the process of verifying that a supplier consistently meets quality, cost, time and quantity requirements. The certification process additionally evaluates the supplier in regard to meeting material specifications and having a documented quality system in place. Process quality controls are examined on the supplier's site, and the customer may be involved in resolving quality issues that arise after certification. A certified supplier guarantees their parts and incoming inspection is typically waived. Materials are delivered to the point of use, bypassing receiving, inspection, and inventory, significantly lowering lead times and costs.

Supplier Consolidation

Supplier consolidation is the process of reducing the number of suppliers for a part. As a company develops relationships with reliable suppliers, it is advisable to reduce the total number of suppliers, maintaining only the reliable ones. To go from multiple sourcing to the preferred single sourcing requires consolidation. Consolidation and ultimately single sourcing are desirable for several reasons. When problems occur with a supplied part, the source of the part is automatically known and the supplier and buyer can work together to resolve the problem. Additionally, having fewer suppliers reduces the variation in production materials.

Vendors and QRP

Vendor-managed inventory is a method of inventory planning and management in which the supplier is responsible for tracking and replenishing customer inventory, including determining order quantities and timing, to reduce costs by reducing inventory while maintaining customer service level

Quick response program (QRP) is a strategy for backward networking retail sales, distribution, production, shipping, and supply to meet product demand quickly and efficiently by sharing point of sale information, usually through electronic data interchange; both lead time and inventory are reduced

An effective QRP requires rapid dissemination of information back through the supply chain for quick response to the customer's needs. Tools required for this rapid information transfer and response include an excellent system for forecasting demand and planning materials and manufacturing, a high level of inventory accuracy, and appropriate technology for data collection at the point of sale, data processing, and quick data transfer. Advantages resulting from an effective QRPs quick customer response time include quicker problem solving, growth in sales and market share due to competitive advantage, and lower costs due to reduced inventory and obsolescence.

On-site vendor/customer representative is supplier staff member located at the customer's site to improve customer service by resolving problems quickly, improving communication, assisting immediately in exploring developmental questions, and anticipating the customer's future needs

An on-site vendor/customer representative is appropriate in situations where the supplier is delivering a substantial amount of goods and/or services to the customer and the supplier and customer have developed a healthy working relationship. Placing a dedicated customer representative at the customer's site is the next logical step in improving the customer service level. On-site customer representatives improve communication between the supplier and customer, quicken the supplier's response time to customer requests, hasten the resolution of problems that arise, and improve the supplier's understanding of customer needs, benefiting both the supplier and the customer.

Communication

Supplier Partnerships

In the past, the primary communication link between the supplier and their customer has been through the supplier's sales representative and the customer's buyer. Anyone else in either company needing to share or obtain information must go through this customer representative-buyer link. The customer's planner had to go through a network of people in order to update orders to reflect schedule changes. In today's manufacturing atmosphere with supplier partnerships, it is recognized that direct communication at all levels is necessary for the two companies to work well as a team. In particular, the customer's and supplier's planners can communicate directly to work together more efficiently and effectively. Building effective communication is necessary for communicating changing demands, maintaining and improving quality, making payments, and agreeing upon packaging.

Transmission of Product Demands and Product Quality

One key communication area is transmitting the product demand and any demand changes from the customer to the supplier. This is usually done electronically and includes both long-term requirements and immediate need for products. Long-term requirements are typically agreed upon through contracts, while short-term needs are filled through product call-offs.

Another key communication area is product quality. Product quality originates at the source, the supplier, who must initially demonstrate and maintain the ability to meet quality, quantity and timing requirements. When this is the case, customers can forego inspecting incoming materials. Any quality problems that arise are resolved jointly by the quality personnel in both companies, eliminating the need for time-consuming practices like rejecting the product and returning it to the supplier.

Payment and Packaging

One key communication area is the payment structure. In a supplier relationship with open, effective communication at all levels, payment for goods can be calculated simply based on the number of containers delivered by the supplier and received by the customer or by back flushing the from the customer's manufacturing output.

Another key communication area is product packaging. By working together and communicating openly about customer needs, the supplier can package the product in standard, reusable containers which hold and protect the materials, contain a suitable quantity for the customer's manufacturing process, fit into the customer's manufacturing flow, and are delivered directly to the customer's point of use. The cost of unnecessary disposable packaging materials is eliminated.

International Communication

Special considerations that apply to communication in international customer-supplier relationships are language and time zone. The issue of language must be considered at all levels. Since English is the international business language, sales and customer service representatives will probably speak it, but building a strong partnership requires communication at all levels. A common language between planners and technical staff of both companies is also important. Customers and suppliers in different time zones also face limitations in when they can communicate. There may be little or no time overlap between the workdays of the two companies, so communication may not be available immediately but must be planned. E-mail communication has eased this problem, but even with e-mail there may be a delay in response. Sending a message one day and receiving a response the next day may be the best-case scenario.

Communication of Data

The speed and ease of transferring data between customer and supplier are important aspects of building a strong, functional partnership. Especially in the cases of vendor-managed inventories (VMI) and quick response programs (QRP) success depends on rapid information flow. Since the speed of data communication is of key importance, technology is essential. Data communication is dependent on technology and changes as technology improves. Commonly used methods to communicate data include fax machines; electronic data interchange (EDI); the internet, including e-mail, intranet, and world wide web; and bar coding. Currently, EDI and the internet are the typical methods.

The following data communication technologies:

- Facsimile (fax): An electronic transmission of a paper document or a computer file.
- Electronic data interchange (EDI): Paperless electronic transmission of documents.
- Internet: A global network of computers connecting computer networks and facilitating the exchange of information through means like e-mail and the worldwide web.
- Electronic mail (e-mail): Passing of messages between individuals through the internet.
- Intranet: An internet-like, private, organization-specific, internal network of computers facilitating the exchange of information.
- Worldwide web: An extensively interlinked portion of the internet displaying information including text, graphics, sound, and animation through the http protocol.
- Bar coding: A method for encoding data in which information is recorded in a combination of bars and spaces for quick and accurate data entry into a computer system.

Electronic Data Communication Technologies in Supplier Relationships

The rise of electronic data communication technologies such as faxes, electronic data interchange (EDI), the internet, e-mail, intranet, the worldwide web and bar coding has greatly increased the speed with which information passes between suppliers and their customers. Instead of depending on the physical transport of paper between sites, electronic data transfer is virtually instantaneous. Suppliers can be informed and updated immediately of customer requirements and changing demands, and lead times are reduced significantly. The world wide web adds the additional facility of advertising products and services and providing online ordering and payment.

Design and Development

Engineering Processes Used

In the manufacturing environment, engineering is the process of designing and developing products and their associated manufacturing processes. The engineering function can be broken down into three categories, design engineering, industrial or manufacturing engineering and maintenance engineering. The role of design engineers is to devise new products with due consideration to the validity of the design and the feasibility of manufacturing it. The role of industrial or manufacturing engineers is to develop a manufacturing process for the product that consistently meets quality and financial goals. The role of the maintenance engineers is to keep the manufacturing machinery operating smoothly and up to standard through planned preventive maintenance to avoid shutdowns due to repairs.

Multidisciplinary Approach

Design and development of products and processes can be viewed as an isolated task, or as a part of the flow of customer service to both external and internal customers. The latter is more effective. Design is best carried out in a multidisciplinary team, including design engineers, industrial engineers, production personnel, quality and value engineers, and production planners. Multidisciplinary design teams minimize engineering changes made later, after the design process, as the product goes into process development and production. Products designed solely by design engineers may be altered significantly by the later engineering functions if those functions were not considered during the design stage. Value engineering involves systematically cutting out process and product waste by considering each function in terms of value added.

Simultaneous Engineering

Simultaneous engineering is a holistic approach to the design process in which all engineering and manufacturing functions and even suppliers and customers are included so that the initial design activity is fully informed and all needs are met. Simultaneous engineering addresses the product's entire life cycle in the design stage. Simultaneous engineering, which can also be referred to as participative design/engineering, increases quality and speed to market and decreases costs. Costs are significantly reduced because engineering changes made in the design stage are much cheaper than engineering changes made later.

Tools and Concepts That Aid in a Speedy, Efficient Design Process

There are several concepts and tools that can be used to aid in the design process. A speedy and effective design process is critical to competing in the marketplace, so tools that facilitate the speed and effectiveness of the design process are invaluable. Minimizing the number of parts in the product, using parts of proven reliability, and using modular design are helpful concepts. Modular design refers to assembling the product from subunits. Statistical process control is a tool that closes the loop between engineering design and process capability so that actual process performance can be used as a basis for costing and engineering decisions. Computer aided design and computer aided engineering are tools that enhance the speed and accuracy of the design process.

Minimization of Parts and Designing for Manufacturability

Minimization of parts is simply the process of standardizing and reducing the number of parts utilized in a product design. Value engineering is an important function in minimizing unnecessary parts. Benefits reaped from minimizing parts include eliminating waste, decreasing lead times, reducing the number of suppliers, increasing flexibility to meet customer needs, and reducing set-up, inventory and production planning costs. Manufacturing performance measures should be considered and included in the design process, particularly minimization of parts.

When product design and process development occur in isolation, there is a costly disconnect between the product and manufacturing. Products are designed which are not feasible to manufacture, resulting in modifications after the design process is complete. Designing for manufacturability closes the gap between product design and manufacture. The manufacture of the product is considered and designed for in the initial product design stage.

QFD

QFD is the process of researching customer needs and desires and incorporating them into the design, development, and production of the product. Through QFD products are designed and manufacturing is executed with the purpose of fulfilling customer expectations. In QFD, the first step in designing a product is ascertaining customer needs. The customer needs then become the specifications to which the product is designed. A manufacturing process is developed and executed with suitable controls to produce the results that the customer requires. In addition to meeting the customer requirements, the product design and manufacturing process should meet the requirements of internal functions such as engineering, materials management, production, quality, business and marketing. A multidisciplinary design team is the best atmosphere for designing, developing, and manufacturing a product that meets customer needs at acceptable cost and quality level.

The first step in identifying customer needs is to determine who the customer is. It can be the next manufacturing work center, another branch within the company, the customer buying the product, and/or the product's end user. After identifying the customer(s), information must be gathered to understand what the customer wants in the product. Satisfaction surveys of current customers, customer complaints received, other means of market research, and internal cross-functional evaluations are all used to understand the needs and desires of potential customers in regard to the product. This information must be carefully examined, digested and ultimately input to the quality and design functions.

QFD Stages for Incorporating Customer Requirements into Product

There are four QFD stages for incorporating the customer requirements into the product. The first stage is product planning. In the product planning stage, the technical product design specifications are developed based on customer requirements. These specifications will then drive the next stage, product design. The product is designed to meet these technical specifications. The third stage is process planning, in which a production process capable of manufacturing the product design is developed. Finally, process control planning occurs. In process control planning, the execution controls for verifying that the designed product meeting the specifications is actually being produced consistently at the required level of quality.

Advantages of the Multidisciplinary Approach

Multidisciplinary Approach

Multidisciplinary approaches to designing and developing products and their associated manufacturing processes include simultaneous engineering, designing for manufacturability, and quality function deployment (QFD). These multidisciplinary approaches yield many competitive advantages for the companies who practice them. These competitive advantages include shorter lead times between a product's initial conception and its market entry, lower total costs for all areas, fewer engineering changes required, better design, improved reliability and higher quality, all due to the multiple inputs. All of these advantages contribute to the ultimate advantage of increased competitiveness for the company.

House of Quality Matrix

The house of quality matrix is used in quality function deployment (QFD). The house of quality is diagrammed as a house built from nine steps. The first step is customer attributes and the customer's product requirements. The second step is the sequence of importance, in which customer attributes are prioritized. The third step is customer perception, how customers view a company's product in comparison to competitor products for each customer attribute. The fourth step is product characteristics, a detailing of how customer attributes could be met in the product design. The fifth step is the product characteristics and customer attributes matrix. The corresponding product characteristic is listed for each customer attribute, including the pros and cons of the product characteristics. The sixth step is the relationships between product characteristics. In this step the interrelationships between the product characteristics are analyzed, including how they affect each other. The seventh step is technical points, including specifications, technical difficulties, costs, and more. The technical points are rated for each product characteristic.

Purchase Orders

Role of Purchase Orders

A purchase order is the contractual agreement between a supplier and their customer establishing the customer's commission of the supplier to provide the specified supplies for the customer. The purchase order can take many forms, including traditional purchase orders, blanket purchase orders, supply contracts managed by vendor scheduling or release systems, just-in-time (JIT) or lean manufacturing environments, consignment stock, and special purchase arrangements like buying capacity, subcontracting, and outside operations. The specific means utilized in a supplier-customer relationship depend on the planning system, execution system, production process and operating philosophy in use.

Traditional Purchase Order

A traditional purchase order is an individual order typically used for supplies to meet a special requirement rather than an ongoing need. A traditional purchase order is created by the buyer and submitted to the supplier, containing order information like product name, description, part number, quantity, price, terms of payment, date required, and delivery method.

Blanket Purchase Order

A blanket purchase order is a long-term agreement between a supplier and purchaser for goods to be provided by the supplier to the purchaser, usually specifying the length of the agreement, the total quantity to be provided and the price. The delivery dates and corresponding delivery quantities can be specified in the agreement, or ordered within the context of the agreement as the need for them arises. Changes can be made to the agreement during its lifespan if necessary; blanket purchase orders were a precursor to supply contracts, but are still used in their own right.

Supply Contract and Vender Scheduling

Supply Contracts

A supply contract is a long-term agreement between a supplier and a purchaser for the supplier to regularly provide goods needed by the purchaser on an ongoing basis. The planning departments of both the supplier and purchaser work together to provide goods as the purchaser requires them. Contracts can include estimated usage, or simply specify that the supplier fulfill whatever requirements arise. The price for goods is set in the contract but price adjustments can be negotiated annually or as necessary. Supply contracts can be managed either through vendor scheduling or the release system.

Vender Scheduling

Vendor scheduling is a method for managing a supply contract in which the purchaser regularly shares their material plan or material requirements schedule and any changes to the plan with the supplier so that the supplier can plan for the long-term future, order supplies for the middle-term future, and manufacture for immediate and near-future needs.

Planning Time Periods Used in Vendor Scheduling

The vendor scheduling method for managing supply contracts divides future planning into three periods. The first period is called Period A or the firm commitment zone. It covers the immediate future. The supplier manufactures these requirements, and the period spans the supplier's lead time. The purchaser is firmly committed to the requirements within this window and will pay for them even if later changes in requirements occur. The second planning window is period B, a middle-future information zone. The supplier uses this requirements information for ordering purposes only. The supplier is committed enough to pay for raw materials associated with these requirements, but does not yet authorize manufacturing. The last planning window, period C, is a distant-future information window. The supplier uses this information for planning purposes only. Production capacity is earmarked, but raw materials are not ordered and manufacturing does not begin.

Release System

Release system is a method for managing a supply contract in which the purchaser issues releases periodically to the supplier that inform the supplier of short-term and long-term needs so that the supplier can plan and execute accordingly; the short-term requirements are filled by the supplier, and the long-term requirements are for planning purposes; an allowable percent change in requirements is typically agreed upon in the supply contract, and issued releases replace their predecessors.

JIT LEANING MANUFACTURING

Just in time (JIT)/lean manufacturing is a production environment in which required materials are delivered to the point of use exactly when they are needed for manufacturing in the quantity required for that manufacturing run; the purchaser provides a schedule for the supplier to follow. Deliveries are scheduled at precise times, and can occur several times per day.

BUYING CAPACITY

Buying capacity is a method in which customers obtain goods through reserving production capacity per period rather than expressing product requirements; as time passes, the customer communicates with the supplier about how the production capacity will actually be used; the supplier is able to plan for the customer's future production while the customer is able to delay finalizing product requirements

OUTSIDE OPERATIONS

Outside operations is the practice of sending manufacturing lots to an external supplier for the performance of one manufacturing operation; outside operations are used when special equipment or processing unavailable internally to the purchaser is required, or when one work center is completely overloaded; outside operations differs from subcontracting in that only one operation is performed and the bulk of manufacturing still occurs internally

DELIVERY

ROLE OF DELIVERY IN SUPPLIER PARTNERSHIPS

The method of product delivery is an important aspect of supplier partnerships. The method of delivery can increase or decrease supplier lead time and cost. Approaches to regular delivery, expedited delivery, batch size, and packaging are all significant. Standard containers eliminate the waste of disposable containers, reduce counting time, and can fit into the manufacturing flow. Different delivery frameworks in use include traditional delivery, just-in-time (JIT) delivery, kanban delivery, point-of-use delivery, and third party logistics. Eliminating or decreasing redundant materials handling, storage and retrieval of materials, incoming verification and inspection, and other unnecessary delivery functions can result in significant savings.

DELIVERY TERMS

Traditional delivery: A method for transporting goods form the supplier to the customer in which the goods arrive with a delivery note, are verified for date and quantity requirements at goods receiving, and are inspected and stored; traditional delivery is a long, expensive process which adds to the lead time and cost.

Just-in-time (JIT) delivery: The frequent arrival of goods required for production in the quantity and at the time required for a manufacturing run; suppliers are certified so no incoming inspection is performed; goods are packaged in standard containers and the number of containers received are tallied per time period and accounts settled accordingly.

Third-party logistics: A delivery method in which the supplier uses an outside company called a third party to handle delivery of goods and other logistics, freeing the supplier to focus on their specialty, manufacturing, through employing a logistics specialist to handle logistics; logistics can include all aspects of warehousing and distribution.

Kanban delivery: A delivery method in which the supplier picks up empty standard containers from the purchaser, refills them, and returns them to the purchaser; an empty standard container serves as the purchaser's authorization to the supplier to deliver another container; kanban delivery can go through goods receiving and incoming inspection or straight to the point of use when the supplier is certified, usually the latter; the number of containers delivered is tallied and accounts are settled per time period.

Point-of-use delivery: A delivery method in which the supplier delivers the goods, usually in standard containers, not to goods receiving but to the point in the manufacturing flow where the goods will be used; the goods are either delivered to the point of use at the time when they are needed for manufacturing, or they are stored at the point of use and pulled from storage as needed; point-of-use delivery provides savings by reducing materials handling such as goods receiving, incoming inspection, counting, and inventory.

Billing

Billing Terms

Accounts payable: The division of a company that manages payments owed by the company; accounts payable can also refer to the outstanding bills the company owes.

Accounts receivable: The division of a company that manages billing and collection of payments owed to the company; accounts payable can also refer to the outstanding bills owed to the company.

Payment period: The length of time following delivery of goods within which payment must be made for those goods; the payment period for accounts receivable has a significant impact on the company's cash flow.

Penalty: Financial costs, usually a percentage of the contract value or bill owed, set to encourage complete and timely fulfillment of transaction agreements; suppliers can suffer a penalty for late completion or delivery, while customers can suffer penalties for late payment.

Holdback percentage: An agreed upon portion of the contracted price for goods and/or services that is retained by the customer for a specified time period following delivery or completion to verify that faults or glitches that arise over time are resolved by the supplier in a satisfactory manner.

Free on board (FOB): A method of sales transaction between the supplier and customer in which the point of time or location in delivery in which ownership transfers from the supplier to the customer is specified; a typical use of FOB would be an international transaction when ownership transfers from the supplier to the customer and payment is made to the supplier by the customer before the goods leave the country of origin to avoid international payment disputes, which can be difficult to resolve.

Sight draft: A company's authorization to a third party like a bank to release payment for goods once the third party has seen the goods; this method is often used in FOB transactions.

How Typical Billing and Payment Methods Have Changed

Traditionally, suppliers have invoiced their customers for goods sold at the time of delivery. The customer verifies the accuracy of the invoice, which it reflects the order placed as well as the actual delivery, and then makes payment. This method is called pay on receipt. With the rise of the just-in-time production environment, payment on receipt became impractical due to the large number of deliveries made. Pay on receipt evolved to weekly or monthly payments made for all deliveries received within the time period. Payment on use is made with consignment stock maintained on the customer's site. The customer draws from the consignment stock as needed for production and pays per time period for the parts used. Pay on production is a method used when no records are kept of deliveries. The customer simply reconstructs the number of parts received from their own production output, and pays accordingly for the supplies used in the goods produced per time period.

Payment Penalties by Suppliers and Their Customers

Payment penalties are financial deterrents built into the agreement between a supplier and a customer. A supplier may impose a financial penalty on the customer for late payment of accounts payable. This financial penalty is typically in the form of a percentage charged per time period that the payment is late. A customer may impose financial penalties on the supplier if the product is not delivered or work is not performed on time. This financial penalty is typically in the form of a dollar amount or percentage of the contract value based on how late to be deducted from the final price paid for goods and/or service. Alternatively, financial incentives can be used such as suppliers giving customers a percentage off bills that are paid early.

Supplier Rating Systems

Supplier rating systems encompass the process of maintaining supplier performance requirements, evaluating the suppliers quantitatively with regard to the supplier performance requirements, and closing the loop with the supplier by transmitting their results back to them. An effective supplier rating system requires clear and timely communication of customer demands to the supplier. Without this, supplier ratings include problems caused by the customer and do not accurately reflect the supplier's performance. In the past, on-time delivery and low cost were the primary benchmarks in rating suppliers. As quality came to the fore in manufacturing, the supplier's quality level eclipsed cost as a benchmark. Finally, the responsiveness of the supplier to the customer has become a benchmark in the current atmosphere of supplier partnerships. There are always differences between companies in supplier ratings due to diversity of industries, operating philosophies and purchasing requirements.

Measuring Supplier Performance

The target for supplier performance is delivery of the product ordered in the required quantity and quality at the specified time and place for a reasonable cost with accurate paperwork. If there is some sort of problem with the order, then the supplier should respond quickly and effectively to solve it. From this target, we can derive the markers of supplier performance: timely delivery of goods, accurate quantity of goods, goods meeting customer specifications, accurate paperwork, and responsiveness, which is quick and effective problem resolution. Gauging supplier performance requires quantitatively tracking the supplier's performance in the following areas: customer service level (defined as the percentage of customer orders met), percentage of orders delivered on time, the percentage of orders delivered complete, percentage of orders delivered in the correct quantity, percentage of orders delivered with acceptable quality, and percentage of scheduled delivery dates changed by the supplier. In a customer-supplier relationship, it is important for the customer to communicate performance measurement results to the supplier so that improvements can be made.

Engineering Change Control

Engineering change control is a technique for managing engineering changes, or changes to a product's bill of materials. In engineering change control, anyone within the company or even a customer can submit engineering change requests to an engineering change order board, or engineering change review board. The board consists of all department managers and is chaired by a high-level company executive. All members of the board receive the change requests in advance and consider them with respect to their own department prior to meeting. The board meets to engage in informed discussion of the change requests and makes a joint decision regarding the change. An engineering change controller serves as the administrator of the process, receiving and distributing change requests, communicating board decisions to change requestors, and disseminating engineering change orders appropriately.

Implementation of Engineering Changes

Engineering changes are implemented by updating the appropriate product bills of material to reflect the change. Since bills of material are the roadmap for manufacturing, their contents should be tightly controlled. Personnel responsible for making approved changes to the bills of material must have access to the bills of material contents, but it should be a small group of people with no connection to production or material handling. It is preferable that bill of material change staff be part of the quality or standards department. Free access to read the bills of material must be readily available, but free access to change bills of material leads to problems.

Communication of Engineering Changes to Suppliers

When a proposed engineering change is officially accepted, an engineering change note or engineering change order is formulated and distributed to all concerned staff and departments within the company, including the planner. The planner then relates the engineering change to the affected suppliers directly or through other means of communication established in the supplier partnership. The supplier uses the information to purchase the correct raw materials and produce parts that line up with the change. Ideally, the supplier should be aware of proposed changes before they are approved and implemented so that they are not caught unaware. Timely communication with the supplier regarding changes is essential to avoid obsolete inventory at every stage and to insure that the supplier meets customer requirements so that the customer's manufacturing is not interrupted.

Procurement Process Communication

For a supplier partnership to function well and meet established goals, the communication of information between the supplier and the customer is essential. One key way to exchange intangible but critical information is through site visits between the customer and the supplier. Direct communication between the two should include the relaying of demands by the customer to the supplier, the promising of orders by the supplier to the customer, notification of delays by the supplier to the customer, and renegotiation of delayed orders. Information technology is an important consideration since it facilitates the communication process.

Site Visits

Site visits are visits made by the customer to the supplier's physical location and by the supplier to the customer's physical location. Through site visits, the visitors learn the site's mode of operation as well as problems encountered. Additionally, there is a personal meeting between the partners, which can generate greater trust and cooperation between them. From visiting the customer, the supplier learns how the customer uses the goods purchased. From visiting the supplier, the customer learns the supplier's manufacturing process, problems, and capability. Information exchanged in site visits is often intangible rather than tangible, but it is valuable nonetheless. Greater understanding between the partners is developed, and ideas are generated that are beneficial to both parties.

Communication of Demand

Communication of demand from the customer to the supplier is the foundation of the customer-supplier relationship. The customer usually informs the supplier of required goods through purchase orders or material requirements schedules. Material requirements schedules typically extend far into the future, making changes inevitable. The customer must inform the supplier not only of the original material schedule but also of changes made to it as time passes. The timeliness of the customer's communication of demand and demand changes is crucial to the supplier's ability to meet those demands and avoid material shortages in the customer's manufacturing operation.

Order Promising

Order promising is the supplier's response to the customer's demand for goods committing to a proposed delivery date for the goods requested. Promised orders are a firm commitment to deliver. Manufacturing resource planning (MRPII) systems with the available-to-promise function are a good way to perform these calculations reliably. The available-to-promise function calculates the amount of uncommitted stock per time period, which is the amount of stock available to promise for that time period. The figures are updated automatically as new orders are entered into the system. The available-to-promise function extends the full length of the master schedule, so order promising can be performed far into the future. A less reliable means of order promising is basing the promised order on the product's lead time without considering available materials for production, available production capacity, or other orders received. It is assumed that as long as there is enough time to manufacture the product then the product can be produced and delivered.

Notification of Delays

Once a supplier realizes that a promised order will not be delivered on time, it is crucial to inform the customer immediately. Delayed orders cause problems for manufacturers, and unexpected delays cause worse problems. Once the delay is known, manufacturing can be planned accordingly, but if a delivery simply fails to show up at the promised time, the supplier's credibility is greatly damaged.

Once a shipment is delayed, the supplier and customer must renegotiate a delivery date. The customer can then plan based on the new delivery date. For the supplier, meeting the renegotiated delivery date is essential. They have already lost some credibility with the customer, and must not make the situation worse.

Information Technology Communication

The role of information technology in communication between the supplier and their customer is pivotal, since the communication itself is pivotal and is facilitated by information technology. One novel approach that can be very effective is for the customer to give the supplier limited access to their internal computerized information system. Then the supplier automatically has the demand information necessary to meet the supplier's needs without extra steps to communicate that information. As schedules and schedule updates are made, the supplier immediately and automatically has access to them. One way to implement this approach is for the supplier to be treated as the customer's work center with work center specific access to company information.

Role of Education and Training

A good manufacturing company aims for continual improvement of their operation. Continual improvement is accomplished by consistently making small changes to improve operation. One factor in maintaining continual improvement is education and training for personnel. Education and training helps personnel overcome fear of and unwillingness to change, while also providing necessary support for personal and corporate growth. Education and training can be provided by both external and internal sources and can cover basic education, technical education, and behavioral education. Specific areas of technical education include all areas of manufacturing, such as product design, quality, the production process, delivery, accounting, and any technology utilized by the company in these fields.

In Supplier Partnerships

Education and training play an important role in supplier partnerships. Similar to internal company dynamics, times of transition are difficult in customer-supplier relationships. Transitions can include supplier delivery changes prompted by the customer, supplier manufacturing changes prompted by the customer, transitions from authoritarian to participative leadership in either, and more. Training is essential to help all workers and leaders understand the motivation for the change, the change itself, and its implementation. Customers commonly invite their suppliers to participate in their internal training programs so that both can grow and move forward together.

Distribution

Distribution is the process of moving finished products and/or service parts from the end of the manufacturing process, through any and all intermediate steps, to the end user of the products and/or service parts. Distribution also includes returning goods to the manufacturer if necessary. Both suppliers and their customers must either perform or outsource the distribution function. Suppliers distribute goods to their customers, and their customers, manufacturers, distribute goods to the end users. Transportation, storage, inventory management, material handling, and information and communication systems can all be aspects of distribution. Distribution can also be called physical distribution.

Order Qualifiers and Winners

Order qualifiers are prerequisites a supplier must meet for a customer to consider doing business with them; price is a typical order qualifier, since it is not usually the most important consideration when choosing a supplier, but a price outside of the customer's range would disqualify the supplier from consideration.

Order winners are supplier characteristics that cause customers to choose that supplier over their competition; order winners can be the price, design or quality of the company's product, the speed or reliability of the company's delivery, or the company's image, flexibility or post-sale service level; companies do not usually focus on more than one or two order winners.

Education and Training Terms

Cross training: he practice of educating individual staff members to perform more than one job, role, or responsibility within the company or within manufacturing; cross training provides flexibility and back-up, both of which contribute to customer responsiveness

Basic education: Training on topics of general knowledge, not related to performance of specific jobs; there is a wide variety of subjects and levels in basic education, beginning with reading and writing; basic education improves worker performance indirectly rather than directly, but still helps employees handle their responsibilities better

Technical education: Training related to the theory and practice of particular job functions or expertise

Behavioral training: Training related to attitudes, communication, people skills, human interactions, etc.; some specific examples of behavioral education topics include management skills, negotiation skills and skills for conducting meetings.

CPIM Practice Test

Want to take this practice test in an online interactive format?
Check out the online resources page, which includes interactive practice questions and much more: **mometrix.com/resources719/cpimdsp**

1. Among the steps that could be taken to ensure a stable manufacturing process are:

a. Ensuring secure and fixed time frames
b. Inputting workloads at the top levels of capacity
c. Ensuring relaxed and temporary time frames
d. Inputting workloads at minimum required capacity levels

2. The unit cost of a product is one factor in production planning. However, the unit cost is a different concept for a merchant retailer than for a manufacturer. The unit cost for a merchant retailer is:

a. The SKU producer cost plus the cost of putting it on the shelf
b. The wage value multiplied by the time it takes for workers who get it on the shelf
c. The actual amount of money spent on making an SKU available for use
d. The price paid and the cost of putting it on the shelf

3. Define SKU, the stock keeping unit.

a. SKU refers to the cost of storing a single unit of a manufactured product
b. SKU refers to characteristics of specific manufactured products but may also refer to services
c. SKU refers to the Universal Product Code, which identifies products by bar codes
d. SKU refers to warranty or information services identified with specific manufactured products

4. The statement that best reflects the importance of SKU in detailed scheduling and planning is:

a. SKU tracks product variations
b. SKU allows inventory managers to count products with electronic scanners
c. SKU tracks production costs as they pertain to inventory management
d. SKU enables market research for future product manufacture

5. In the process of detailed scheduling and planning, managers discover that manufacturing SKU item 983742B requires an unusually high 25% of management supervisory time, compared with only 5% of supervisory time for popular SKU item 983742G.

a. Planners and schedulers should discontinue SKU item 983742B
b. Planners and schedulers should add 20% to the acquisition cost of SKU983742B
c. Planners and schedulers should fire the production supervisor
d. Planners and schedulers should streamline the process for manufacturing SKU 983742B

6. The amount of WIP, or work in progress, __________.

a. Decreases as lead times increase
b. Increases as lead times increase
c. Bears no relationship to lead times
d. Decreases in make-to-order manufacturing

7. Define MRO as it pertains to factory production.

a. MRO refers to maintenance, repair, and operating supplies
b. MRO refers to the software used to track and account for scheduled repair and maintenance that is part of planning lead times
c. MRO refers to corrective and preventive maintenance on equipment used in the manufacturing process
d. All of the above

8. The technique by which a manufacturing company makes decisions about ordering materials and components needed for manufacture is called:

a. The inventory management strategy
b. The materials procurement schedule
c. The order point system
d. Order review methodology

9. The accounting and auditing department of a major electronics manufacturer determines that profit margins are 2% lower than originally stated, even after thorough examination of the entire process. The cause might be:

a. Fluctuation inventory
b. Anticipation inventory
c. Operating supplies
d. Consigned stock

10. Obsolete inventory is different from excess inventory in that:

a. Obsolete inventory is typically written off as a loss, but excess inventory has other uses
b. Excess inventory has carrying costs, whereas obsolete inventory does not
c. Excess inventory is typically reworked, whereas obsolete inventory is sent back to the supplier
d. Materials planners must find a new use for obsolete inventory; excess inventory can generally be sent back to the supplier

11. MRP logic is often referred to as a "backward process." Where does MRP logic begin?

a. MRP logic begins at the beginning
b. MRP logic begins by responding to the requirements of the master production schedule
c. MRP logic begins with forecast demand and target date for finished product(s)
d. MRP logic begins with materials purchasing

12. The statement that best explains the relationship between the MRP method of order review and the MPS is:

a. MRP functions independently of the MPS
b. Materials requirements planning is used to set the master production schedule
c. Planners can safely assume that MRP will accommodate the master production schedule
d. MRP uses the master production schedule, the bills of material, the current inventory records, open purchase orders, and other data to determine material schedules and priorities

13. The statement that best explains the purpose of target inventory level as it relates to the periodic review system of ordering is:

a. New orders are based on the sum of demand during lead time and the review cycle, plus safety stock, in order to meet predetermined target inventory levels
b. Orders for the same number of parts are placed at irregular time intervals to meet variable target inventory levels
c. The quantity of ordering is always the same but occurs at different time periods, depending on the target inventory levels
d. Predetermined target inventory levels are fixed, as are the amounts ordered

14. Materials ordering systems are selected on the basis of certain assumptions. The assumptions made regarding the order point system of ordering are:

a. Demand for the inventory item is constant and independent, and stock should be replenished when used
b. Demand for inventory stock is variable and dependent, so new materials orders are made in fixed amounts
c. The amount of new material orders and demand will always vary and are interdependent
d. The timing of ordering is constant, but demand is independent

15. In the two-bin system of a materials order review system:

a. One bin is used for materials currently in use; the second is used to replenish dminishing levels in the first
b. One bin is used for materials currently in use; the second is empty until new demand figures are received, when it is filled and sealed
c. One bin is used for materials currently being used; the second is a sealed bin that represents the average demand during lead time plus safety stock
d. The sealed reserve bin is used only if work stations run out of stock; the first bin is constantly replenished to "fill" lines

16. Batching rules must be applied to the generic lot-sizing techniques of factory production because:

a. It is always best to order the same amounts of material at varying periods of time
b. Lot sizing derives from the planning stages of factory production but must be further fine-tuned by the applicaton of batching rules that bring theory into practice
c. Factory orders must be tailored to factory capacity more than any other factor
d. Batches move more easily through work centers than do lots

17. Manufacturing order quantities are most often limited by the supplier because:

a. The supplier is always right
b. Customer orders are an unreliable planning component
c. Of space and weight restrictions, setup costs, order processing times
d. Of all of the above

18. The purpose of applying statistical data to the maintenance of safety stock is that:

a. Safety stock levels can accurately reflect statistical demand levels
b. Supplies of material and demand can be predicted statistically
c. Reliable safety stock levels can be measured as a percentage of total production
d. Statistical safety stock is a method for calculating the quantity of safety stock to keep on hand to protect against statistical fluctuations in supply of materials and demand for products

19. In the statistical stock formula "MAD=(ABSUM/N)," the symbol "ABSUM/N refers to:

a. The cumulative sum of absolute deviations between forecast and actual demand in the N number of time periods
b. The sum of absolute deviations between safety stock levels and actual demand in the N number of time periods
c. The number of standard deviations used to provide the desired finished goods service level expressed numerically
d. The number of mean average deviations used to provide the desired finished goods service level expressed numerically

20. In planning the amount of safety stock that should be maintained, it is sometimes necessary to factor in the concept of safety lead time. Safety lead time may be defined as:

a. A time buffer added to calculated lead time to protect against lead time fluctuations and ensure that required material is available when needed
b. A time buffer added to the actual lead time to protect against lead time fluctuations and ensure that required material is available when needed
c. A time buffer added into both calculated or actual lead time to protect against lead time fluctuations to ensure that required materials are available when needed
d. All of the above

21. When manufacturing entirely new products, the method of setting safety stock is most likely to be:

a. Time-period safety stock
b. Statistical safety stock
c. Fixed safety stock
d. Lot-for-lot safety stock

22. The statement that best describes the use and purpose of tracking signals is:

a. Tracking signals are emitted from RFID transmitters used to track the movement of materials or components needed for manufacture.
b. Tracking signals are computations that attempt to determine when forecast demand is inaccurate and unreliable.
c. Tracking signals are computations of the difference between forecast and actual demand.
d. Tracking signals are computations of the speed at which material flows through a production phase.

23. Of FIFO inventory evaluation methods, it may be said that:

a. Inventory is valued at the current price and reflects inflationary increases in the price of materials
b. Inventory is valued at the wholesale value of materials sold to the manufacturing customer and is independent of material costs
c. Inventory is valued at an average price beginning with the cost of the first material order and ending with the last
d. Inventory is valued at the price paid for it and does not reflect inflationary increases in the price of materials

24. Of LIFO inventory evaluation methods, it may be said that:

a. Inventory is valued at the average price and does not reflect inflationary increases in the price of materials
b. Inventory is valued at the wholesale value of materials sold to the manufacturing customer and is independent of material costs
c. Inventory is valued at the actual cost of the last material ordered and reflects the impact of inflationary pressures on profits.
d. Inventory is valued at the price paid for it and does not reflect inflationary increases in the price of materials

25. When purchased raw materials are transferred to other work locations or stations within the same manufacturing corporation, the concept of "transfer costing" comes into play. The best description of "transfer costing" is that it is:

a. A method of inventory accounting in which materials are used in the reverse order in which they are received
b. A method of inventory accounting that presumes that materials are used in the order sequence in which they are received
c. A method of inventory valuation based on the actual cost, with transportation and handling costs added to the value
d. A method of inventory costing that is chosen on the basis of tax accounting treatment

26. The description that best explains the "weighted moving average" of inventory evaluation is:

a. The weighted moving average method of inventory evaluation averages the cost of all purchased inventory components and materials over a one-year period
b. The weighted moving average method of inventory evaluation measures the average cost of all materials purchases over a three-year period
c. The weighted moving average method of inventory evaluation averages the cost of all purchased inventory components and materials
d. The weighted moving average method of inventory evaluation measures the amount of inventory purchased at intervals in different time periods and averages them

27. The method of inventory valuation that is theoretical and based on inventory planning targets is called:

a. The LIFO method
b. The FIFO method
c. The weighted moving average method
d. The standard costing method

28. Which of the following methods of costing would be more likely used by a business oriented more toward providing customer services than the manufacture of large quantities of products?

a. Project costing
b. Actual costing
c. Process costing
d. Standard costing

29. The equivalent unit of production is best described as:

a. Value derived from tracking the individual cost of manufacturing single items and multiplying that by the number of items produced
b. Value added to the cost of manufactured items by summing the cost of the total process and dividing the sum by the number of items processed
c. The average cost per unit
d. Half the average cost per unit multiplied by the number of units in a batch

30. The primary human factors that have the most impact on inventory accuracy are:

a. Necessary counting tools and equipment such as RFID
b. Adequate containers and storage space for materials and products
c. Employees who must bear responsibility for inventory accuracy and who are sufficiently trained to manage the tools and physical components of inventory accuracy
d. All of the above

31. An accounting system that assigns costs to specific tasks in the production process is called:

a. Product costing
b. Standard costing
c. Process costing
d. Job order costing

32. Activity-based cost accounting is growing in popularity in comparison with traditional cost accounting because:

a. Activity-based cost accounting lends itself to large volume product manufacturing
b. Traditional cost accounting categories like wages, utility costs, maintenance, and depreciation often fail to capture hidden manufacturing costs
c. Activity-based cost accounting eliminates the record-keeping requirements of traditional accounting categories
d. Activity-based cost accounting lends itself to low-volume luxury goods manufacturing

33. Popular methods of ensuring inventory count accuracy are:

a. Sampling, double counting, and verifying
b. RFID counting and machine data recording
c. Photorecording, RFID counting, and dedicated inventory managers
d. All of the above

34. The role of the inventory auditor(s) in annual inventory accounting is:

a. To make certain the inventory count is done accurately
b. To reconcile actual inventory to inventory documents and records
c. Create categories of inventory costing that will be used on the annual report
d. To determine the asset value of WIP

35. The statement that best describes cycle counting as an alternative to annual inventory counting is:

a. Cycle counting provides that inventory counting responsibilities are shifted to upper-level management
b. Cycle counting relies on personnel outside the production process to count inventory
c. Cycle counting is always done on a daily basis and so is more accurate
d. Cycle counting is an ongoing process of physically counting storage materials according to a predetermined schedule

36. For inventory management personnel considering adaptation of RFID, the primary concern(s) would be:

a. Whether to implement the process at shipping and receiving points or elswhere
b. Cost and the need for accuracy
c. Interference risk from other radio frequencies in the environment
d. Data sharing

37. Ignoring the costs, a key advantage of RFID technology in inventory tracking is that:

a. It traces movement in real time and real location, rather than at specific counting points such as the shipping and receiving area of a manufacturing firm
b. RFID makes huge amounts of data available for analysis
c. RFID can determine the expiration dates of products subject to spoilage
d. All of the above

38. Can RFID be used in manufacturing supply replenishment?

a. No, it is too expensive to be used for replenishment
b. Yes, use of raw material or component data can be sent to a central control center to trigger replenishment, even to externally linked suppliers
c. Yes, it is most effectively used in the manufacture of small volumes of luxury items
d. No, because it is no more accurate than manual two-bin systems, and much less expensive

39. Among the criteria that can be used to evaluate customer service quality are:

a. Stockout percentages, backlog percentages
b. Safety stock inventory, warranty costs, and friendly service
c. Item and dollar volume quantity of sales
d. Number of product returns

40. By what criteria does service level measure customer service?

a. Service level means to accommodate a customer in the transaction of sales and help in the use of products
b. Service level measures customer service by means of product satisfaction surveys
c. Service level measures the percentage of orders, order line items, or order dollar amounts that the company fills successfully according to the customer's required quality, quantity, and time table
d. Service level criteria include safety factors, backlog, responsiveness, quality, and cost of service

41. How is inventory maintenance enhanced by selecting a control group for inventory purposes?

a. A control group is a selected sample of products sometimes used to find and remedy problems of inventory accuracy
b. A control group is a select team of people entrusted with the task of ensuring inventory accuracy
c. A control group refers to the process of counting all inventory items held in storage and comparing the count with existing records and documents
d. A control group refers to the inventory management team assigned to enhance inventory accuracy

42. The largest cost in guaranteeing a high level of customer service is

a. Order taking
b. Backlogged orders
c. Maintaining sufficient inventory levels
d. Reponsiveness

43. To determine the appropriate levels of safety stock, producers of goods must:

a. Use the trial and error method
b. Ask customers to set the levels of safety stock held in inventory
c. Obtain the number of standard deviations or mean average deviations necessary to ensure the desired percentage of customer service level from a chart or table
d. Base safety stock on the amount of forecast demand and multiply by lead time days

44. Inventory accuracy target tolerances must be at a percentage to be feasible. That percentage is:

a. 90%
b. 95%
c. 70 %
d. 75%

45. In the context of manufacturing, the term "independent demand" means:

a. Demand that must be predicted or forecast
b. Internal demand from assembly line operations
c. Demand from retail customers at shopping outlets
d. All of the above

46. In the area of materials planning, "lumpy demand" refers to:

a. High demand for materials during batching followed by a period of zero demand for additional batches
b. Ademand for materials that, if graphically depicted, would be low at each end of the time period for manufacturing and bulging in the middle
c. A demand for hard-to-handle materials that incur additional inventory costs
d. A high level of customer demand that cannot be met by production capacity

47. The types of information necessary for successful inventory planning process are:

a. Inventory, master schedule, and engineering spec data
b. Master schedule data and physical inventory balance
c. Bills of material, purchase order, and WIP balances
d. All of the above

48. An inventory type that does not meet specification requirements will be categorized as:

a. Floor stock
b. Quarantined stock
c. Critical stock
d. Isolated stock

49. The "projected available balance," which appears on the inventory stock status report, refers to:

a. Items in stock and available for use
b. Current stock, open orders, and planned orders
c. Production materials available on the floor but that does not meet specification standards
d. Critical stock

50. Name three inventory performance criteria that can be measured.

a. Current stock, open orders, planned orders
b. Projected available balance, projected on-hand balance, and future stock
c. Critical stock, floor stock, and quarantined stock
d. Inventory turnover, customer service level, and inventory accuracy

51. A newly hired operations manager needs to get an overall picture of a popular consumer product the company assembles. Assuming that the new manager has access to all computer data files, the best place to look is:

a. The bills of materials file
b. The work center file
c. The item master data file
d. The routing file

Answer Key and Explanations

1. A: Answer choice "a" is correct because secure and fixed time frames for manufacturing are necessary for the stability of the manufacturing process. A stable process ensures profitability and overall efficiency. Secure and fixed time frames for various phases of manufacture are at the center of detailed planning and scheduling. While a fixed system may have an in-built capacity for change, a realistic adherence to capacity requirements will prevent bottlenecks and system overload.

2. D: The correct answer is "d." For the merchant retailer, unit cost is a relatively easy matter. The retailer (or wholesaler) pays a price to the manufacturing supplier for delivery of the product. The only thing to be added is the cost of making it available to consumers and whatever costs are associated with temporary storage. For a manufacturer, a unit cost is a more complex matter, since production costs can vary according to the efficiency and planning of the manufacturing process.

3. B: The correct answer is "b." The SKU is different from the bar code and is used for product and product family identification. The number and alpha string of the SKU identifier will provide information regarding color, size, configuration, and other characteristics that render the product different from those that appear identical or nearly so. There is an increasing tendency to include warranty or service information coding in the SKU. Sometimes SKUs are assigned to activities rather than products.

4. C: While all of the answer choices apply, the best answer is "c." SKU is a means of tracking productive profitability. When an SKU is assigned to a finished product, the cost of manufacture is a known factor attached to it, as is the profit margin when it is sold to retailers/wholesalers. Storage, handling, and sales costs can be tracked from that point onward to help manufacturers make decisions on future manufacturing processes. If SKU 983742B sells poorly, while 983742G sells out repeatedly, planners and schedulers can adjust manufacturing in the direction of greater profitability by making more of the more desired consumer item.

5. B: The best answer is "b." There are many good reasons why the manufacture of one product might require more supervisory attention than that of another. Firing the supervisor for practical and necessary production expenses is not a solution. It is true that the planners might look at streamlining the process, but the cost of the product is already a fact. That cost, an extra 20%, must be added to the product acquisition (manufacturing) cost, since the main purpose of tracking SKU983742B is to ensure profitability. It may very well be that SKU983742B sells well at the high price and cost.

6. B: The correct answer is "b." Longer lead times and make-to-order manufacturing both tend to increase the amount of work in progress. In make-to-order, the increased volume of work in progress is intended because the family composition of different groups may require holding work until orders are received for completion. With regard to longer lead times required by some kinds of manufacturing, there is more unfinished material in the pipeline, a factor that must be accounted for in inventory costing.

7. D: The correct answer "d," all of the above is. Maintenance, repair, and the operating supplies necessary to perform preventive and corrective maintenance are a necessary part of planning and must be scheduled into production activity. In complex manufacturing operations, there is a need to control this process with software that monitors MRO and constructs reports of equipment failure. The measurement of MTBF (mean-time between failures) is an important function of detailed scheduling and planning.

8. D: Order review methodology, answer choice "d," is the technique by which a manufacturing company makes decisions about ordering materials and components needed for manufacture. The order point system is just one of many order review methods. Other choices in ordering include materials requirements planning, the periodic review system, time phased order point systems, and simple visual systems, where ordering is done by sight. In more complex systems, ordering is a computerized process, though simplified manual supply ordering techniques work in many cases.

9. C: The best answer is "c," one could make an argument that any of the costs associated with the answer choices are reasonable. Fluctuation inventory and anticipation inventory are directed toward specific purposes, and there is a cost attached to maintaining any inventory. However, the cost of these, just as with the costs of consigned stock, is known and visible factors. The element of manufacturing most likely to be missed is MRO and/or operating supplies. A lack of controls on these can eat into profits. This problem is often addressed by charging the costs first to factory overhead and then input into the individual product costing system.

10. A: Knowledge of the different types of inventory would lead you to choose "a" as the correct answer. Obsolete inventory is most often written off as a loss, though sometimes salvage can account for marginal recoupment of loss. It is difficult to find uses for material parts or components that are truly obsolete. Excess inventory, whether in the form of finished products or raw materials, can be sold to other customers. All inventory has carrying costs, however, and those costs must be factored into the cost of inventory.

11. C: MRP logic begins at the end, with the forecast demand and target date for the finished product, and works backward through each required item toward the beginning, the raw materials, with the view of meeting the master production schedule. If there is not enough of an item to meet the demand on time, then orders are checked to see if there will be enough. If enough have been ordered, then the arrival date is checked. If the order will not arrive on time, then the order is rescheduled. If the item has not been ordered, then an order is placed. MRP logic applies to purchased items as well as parts manufactured within the company. This sequence is repeated for all materials used in production, from end to beginning.

12. D: The correct answer is "d." The material requirements planning (MRP) method of order review is based on prioritization of the type and amount of materials to be ordered and the timing Of order placement and delivery—all determined by the master production schedule (MPS). The overall purpose of the material requirements planning (MRP) system is to use the MPS, the bills of material, the current inventory records, open purchase orders, and other data to determine material schedules and priorities for both purchased and manufactured materials so that materials will be timely available to achieve MPS levels.

13. A: The correct answer is "a." Inventory reviews occur periodically, and the amounts ordered are based upon the sum of demand during lead times, plus review times, plus safety stock. The number ordered is basically the demand since the previous review, which is the amount of materials or components necessary to restore the TIL. Like the order point system, the periodic review system assumes that demand is constant and independent and that items that have been used for manufacture should be replenished.

14. A: The correct answer is "a." The order point system assumes that demand for the inventory item is constant and independent and that stock should be replenished when used. In the order point system, orders for additional inventory are made when the number of items available for use has decreased to a predetermined order point. The number of items available for use is the amount of material in inventory combined with the amount on order. The order point system is also called the variable cycle, fixed order quantity system because the time between orders varies, but the quantity of the order is always the same.

15. C: The correct answer is "c." The two-bin system is an organized visual review system in which there are two bins holding the inventory item. One bin is open for use, while the other bin is sealed; the sealed bin holds the average demand during lead time plus the safety stock. When the open bin runs out, it is replaced with the contents of the sealed bin, at which time a new order is placed. The contents of the reserve sealed bin should be sufficient to last until the new order arrives, at which point another sealed reserve bin is reestablished.

16. B: The best answer is "b." Lot-sizing techniques produce a theoretical number of items to be ordered, but these theoretical lot sizes are not necessarily feasible. Batching rules bring theory into practice. Examples of batching rules are minimum order quantity and maximum order quantity. The minimum order quantity rule sets the smallest number of parts that can be ordered. This minimum is usually required by the supplier to cover setup costs incurred in filling the order. The maximum order quantity rule sets the largest number that can be ordered at one time.

17. C: The best answer is "c"; in the ideal world, order quantities would be perfectly matched to demand and to supplier limitations. In order to have materials or components timely delivered, production schedulers must work within the capacity and other restrictions of suppliers. Maximum order quantity can be set for reasons such as space and weight restrictions and lead times. Minimum order sizes are sometimes determined by supplier setup and processing costs.

18. D: The correct answer is "d." Statistical safety stock is a method for calculating the quantity of safety stock to keep on hand to protect against statistical fluctuations in supply of materials and demand for products. The formula for statistical safety stock is SS=S*SF*[Sqrt(L/FP)] or SS=1.25*MAD*SF*[Sqrt(L/FP)], where SS is the safety stock, S is the standard deviation, SF is the safety factor, L is the lead time, FP is the forecast time period, and MAD is the mean absolute deviation.

19. A: The correct answer is "a." ABSUM is the cumulative sum of absolute deviations between forecast and actual demand in time periods considered and N is the number of time periods. The formula is associated with the formula for determining the levels of statistical safety stock to protect against fluctuations of supply of materials and demand for products. The formula for statistical safety stock is SS=S*SF*[Sqrt(L/FP)] or SS=1.25*MAD*SF*[Sqrt(L/FP)], where SS is the safety stock, S is the standard deviation, SF is the safety factor, L is the lead time, FP is the forecast time period, and MAD is the mean absolute deviation.

20. D: Answer "d," all of the above. The time buffer of safety lead time may be added into either calculated or actual lead times to protect against lead time fluctuations. The purpose is to ensure that required materials are available when needed for manufacture. Safety lead time is used when the supplier is habitually late or inconsistent with order timing; it is also useful in place of safety stock when items are ordered as needed and not stocked. Another term for safety lead time is safety time.

21. C: The correct answer is "c." Fixed safety stock is a predetermined quantity of safety stock set without respect to demand, demand variation, usage, or supplier dependability. Fixed safety stock quantities can be used for new products and in other special cases. The reason a fixed safety stock technique is used is because there is no baseline history that can be used to predict surges in demand. Therefore, a fixed quantity is set as a precaution against running out. Later, a baseline history can establish a more accurate method of setting safety stock limits.

22. B: The correct answer is "b." Tracking signals are used to monitor the accuracy of the forecast demand in relation to the actual demand, and signal when the forecast demand may be inaccurate and remedied by adjustment. The tracking signal is calculated as follows: TS=(SUM/MAD., where MAD=(ABSUM/N); TS is the tracking signal, SUM is the algebraic sum of deviations between forecast and actual demand during the time periods considered, MAD is the mean average deviation, ABSUM is the sum of absolute deviations between forecast and actual demand during the time periods considered, and N is the number of time periods considered. The forecast demand must be revisited when the tracking signal reaches positive or negative four.

23. D: Answer "d" is the correct answer. First-in-first-out (FIFO) inventory valuation is based on the price actually paid for the inventory (actual individual cost per item). Since the materials should be used in the order they were received, and valued at the price actually paid for them, the inventory values of stock being used does not reflect the price increase until the older, cheaper stock is used up. FIFO delays the effect of inflation, maximizing profits in the short term. The inference to be drawn from this, as it pertains to plannning, is that the internal cost of goods sold less accurately reflects the current market situation than the LIFO method.

24. C: Answer "c" is correct. In the LIFO (last-in-first-out) method of inventory valuation, the valuations more accurately reflect inflationary price increases in the cost of raw materials or component parts. Accounting for inflation or deflation in the method of valuing raw materials costs leads to more accurate profit projections. If the last prices paid are higher than the materials purchased previously, the profit projections would be on the conservative side. If the last prices paid are less expensive than the prices previously paid, there is still better accuracy in the certainty that inventory valuation was conducted and profits projected on actual and real prices, rather than more optimistic price projections.

25. C: Option "c" is the correct answer. Transfer costing is a method of inventory valuation used to value inventory that has been transferred within the company without being sold. The economic value assigned to the transferred material is usually the actual or standard cost, plus handling and transportation costs. It is interesting to note that tax accounting needs sometimes accounts for choosing between LIFO and FIFO inventory valuation. From an asset standpoint, it may be sometimes be favorable to have higher inventory valuations and lower valuations at other times.

26. C: The correct answer "c." In the weighted moving average method of inventory valuation, value is assigned to inventory based on the average value of all stock purchased and held. Inflation, deflation, and other price changes are spread out through all of the current inventory stock. Weighted moving average methodology can't be applied to one or three-year time periods because it must be paired with production schedules, not calendar time. The weighted moving average is recalculated with each new batch of inventory by adding the cost of the new items to the total value of the items already in stock, and then dividing by the total number of items (old and new).

27. D: The correct answer is "d." The standard costing method of inventory valuation is based on the target or theoretical cost of materials, labor, and overhead. The standard cost is calculated by determining the current actual cost at the beginning of a predetermined time period (usually a year or a quarter), estimating what the actual cost will be at the end of the time period (accounting for inflation and other price changes), and averaging the time period starting cost and estimated ending cost. This average is the standard cost. Each time the standard cost is recalculated, current inventory is revalued to the new standard cost.

28. A: The best answer is "a." Project costing is a method of inventory valuation in which actual costs are tracked for an overall project, and not for individual products or processes. Project costing is the right choice for businesses that do not have a manufactured product but instead provide services. The project costing method is used in industries oriented toward customer service, where projects are highly specific, not repeated, and geared toward individual customers. The project cost includes all actual or standard costs incurred while executing the project. In the execution of some projects or services, project costing may be combined with actual costing, tracked and documented as they occur.

29. B: The correct answer is "b." Equivalent unit of production is a concept used in process costing. It refers to the total cost of manufacturing products, obtained by averaging or summing the total cost of a process and dividing that by the number of items processed. Until a product is completed and held in finished inventory, the WIP is sometimes arbitrarily assigned a value equal to 50% of an equivalent unit of production.

30. C: The correct answer is "c." The hiring and implementation of personnel can have a great impact on inventory accuracy. Personnel must be properly trained in how to execute the job; they must be willing to assume responsibility for inventory accuracy, and must be entrusted with appropriate authority to access and tabulate locked stores, and to manage modern systems of documentation control. Modern systems of documentation control may involve training in the use of complex data collection tools and the transmission of data by electronic means to various nodes in the manufacturing structure. In addition, suitable personnel must be familiar with methods of storing dangerous or nonconforming materials.

31. D: Job order costing, answer "d," is the correct answer. Job order costing is an accounting system which assigns costs to specific tasks in the production process. Job order costing is independent of accounting cut-off dates and costs are carried along with the location of the products. Costs are carried in the specific task category until the product moves to the finished goods inventory. The WIP, at the end of the monthly period, equals the sum of costs attributable to each unfinished work order.

32. B: Answer choice "b" is correct in stating that traditional cost accounting categories often fail to capture hidden costs of manufacture. Manufacturing whether it is high or low volume is irrelevant to the increasing use of ABC methods. The advantage of activity-based costing is that it shifts manufacturing control points so as to apportion resources to activities of the highest priority, capturing the cost of those activities. Manipulation of traditional cost accounting categories does not have a great impact in making a process more efficient. An activity like order picking, for example, may involve a group of related products, the measurement of which, by traditional means, would be lost to accounting.

33. A: Answer "a" is the correct one. Methods for verifying count accuracy during periodic or annual inventory include sampling, double counting, and verifying. In sampling, a few of the inventory items are counted a second time to ensure overall accuracy. In double counting, all materials are counted two times by different individuals or teams to ensure accuracy. In verifying, there is an additional person(s) attached to the counting team to make sure items and locations are not missed, and that the results are accurately recorded.

34. B: The correct answer is "b." It is the job of the inventory auditor(s) to reconcile a company's actual inventory to existing inventory documents and records. Internal inventory records and documents are usually at variance with inventory because some part of actual inventory may become lost, erroneously fabricated, missed in counting, pilfered, or deteriorated in storage. Auditing is carried out through annual inventory counting events and by cycle counting. Many companies require a thorough physical count of all inventory materials each year.

35. D: The correct answer is "d." Cycle counting is an ongoing process of physically counting storage materials according to a predetermined schedule. Cycle counting may be done at variable time intervals, as suits the type of manufacturing being done. Usually, the more used or higher value production items are counted more often, while lower value items may be counted on a less frequent basis. Cycle counting is most effective when it is done by persons specially trained and dedicated to the task.

36. C: The best answer is "c." Cost and the need for accuracy are primary concerns. Data sharing with various nodes and interference risk are elements that can be easily addressed and remedied. On the other hand, RFD is comparatively expensive technology. The high cost of an initial investment in RFD must be balanced against the benefits obtained. Does the need for accuracy justify the cost of RFD? What are the true costs of an RFID installation? RFID wafers or chips can currently be programmed with varying amounts of data. The more specialized the data, the more expensive the wafer. The cost of RFID readers and translators must also be considered.

37. D: The best answer is "d." RFID has broad advantages so long as the cost of RFID implementation can be justified. RFID makes huge amounts of data available for analysis, and RFID wafers can be programmed to display whatever data are sought, even such abstruse data as expiration dates. The more complex the data displayed by an RFID chip, however, the higher the cost of implementing such a system. One of the greatest advantages is that even simple RFID chips will indicate location and movement in the immediate period.

38. B: Choice "b" is correct; the use of raw material or component data can be sent to a central control center to trigger replenishment, even to externally linked suppliers. With regard to assembly stages of manufacturing, RFID can identify irregularities of materials flow and point the way toward the "leaning" of materials in a manufacturing flow process. As such, it is an ideal tool of analysis and remediation for manufacturing bottlenecks. Programmed RFID tags can track material flow in such a way as to react with plus or minus deviation settings to trigger a variety of corrective actions.

39. A: The right answer is "a." A manufacturer should keep a good account of stockout and backlog percentages as a measure of service to the customer. The other answer options are more selective and may or may not indicate customer satisfaction trends. Firms should pay attention to product returns, but these may derive from factors other than poor service to customers. The best quantitative indicators of customer service are stockout and backlog percentages, as these are concrete reasons that may lead to lost business.

40. C: The correct answer is "c." Service level is only a part of customer service, with "customer service" being the more encompassing term. Service level is quantitative, not subjective, as are some elements of customer service. Service levels are measured by determining the percentage of orders, order line items, or order dollar amounts that the company fills successfully according to the customer's required quality, quantity, and time table. In the case of industries with ready-made products, the percentage may be calculated based on items in stock when the order is received.

41. A: The correct answer is "a." The use of a control group can be used to enhance inventory accuracy by physically counting a predetermined set of inventory items at regular, frequent intervals in order to uncover and alleviate inventory errors quickly in situations where inventory accuracy is low. Once problem areas are identified, improvements can then be made to the overall inventory accuracy based on findings in the control group. A control group is a method for highlighting problems with inventory accuracy, rather than a method for maintaining accuracy.

42. C: The best answer is "c," although all of the answer choices result in costs. The biggest challenge is to maintain inventory levels that will prevent stockouts and backlogged orders. Too many stockouts or backlogged orders result in lost business and shrinking profits. Maintaining appropriate levels of inventory increases costs of service, however. "Cost of service" refers to the financial cost associated with customer service levels. Cost of service consists primarily of the cost of inventory necessary to maintain the desired service level.

43. C: The correct answer is "c"; the use of calculations involving both standard deviations and mean average deviations have resulted in tables or charts in which the desired percentage level of customer service can be obtained. Customer service levels must always be balanced against the costs of maintaining inventory to ensure profitability. When charts are unavailable, software programs like Excel can calculate standard deviation. Sometimes, forecast demand is used in place of standard deviation when safety stock is to be calculated.

44. B: While the goal is always 100% accuracy, the tolerance level of 95% guarantees system feasibility, so answer "b" is correct. Inventory accuracy is a measure of the percentage of stock items whose inventory counts on record fall within the tolerance level of the actual number in stock. In computerized inventory management systems, inventory accuracy targets must be 100% in order to achieve the minimum 95% accuracy necessary for the system to be feasible; otherwise, there would be an unreasonable number of inventory excesses and shortages.

45. A: Answer option "a" is correct, since, within the context of manufacturing, independent demand is unrelated to internal manufacturing activity and must be projected and forecast. Independent demand is the amount of finished goods that will be necessary to meet customer orders in projected time periods. Independent demand is what sets and determines "dependent demand," that is, the materials or components that will be necessary to complete assembly of finished products.

46. A: Answer option "a" is correct; "lumpy demand" is irregular, discontinuous, uneven demand. Lumpy component demand is created by finished goods or assembly characterized by periods of high and steady demand alternating with periods of zero demand batching. In other words, all components necessary for the entire batch are demanded at one time, followed by a period of no demand that lasts until the next manufacturing batch requires the associated component parts. Lumpy assembly or finished goods demand may also be created by customers who vary greatly in their ordering habits or end items that are seasonal in nature.

47. D: Answer "d" is correct, as all of the data in question must be obtained in order to plan a successful inventory management process. Having complete, accurate, and up-to-date data is essential to the inventory planning process. Bills of material, purchase order records, work in progress balances, and physical inventory balances must all be maintained accurately, completely, and as changes occur so that neither material shortages nor material excesses result from material resource planning decisions based on faulty information. Work in progress data are especially challenging to locate and maintain in the production environment.

48. B: Answer "b" is correct; materials isolated from regular inventory because they do not meet customer or manufacturing quality specifications are "quarantined." It is one of the many categories that may be found on the "inventory stock status report." Other categories on the inventory stock status report are: stock on hand, open orders, demand history, critical or free stock, projected available balance, projected on-hand balance, floor stock, stafety stock, and year-to-date demand.

49. B: Answer option "b" is the correct answer. Projected available balance refers to the quantity of stock that will be available in the future and includes current stock, open orders, and planned orders. We must be careful to distinguish between "projected available balance" and "projected on-hand balance," the quantity of stock that will be available in the future but that includes only current stock and open orders, and not planned orders.

50. D: The correct answer is "d." The question asks for performance measurement applicable to overall inventory. Inventory turnover, inventory accuracy, and customer service level percentages can be easily measured and numerically represented as overall indications of inventory performance. The other answer choices can be counted but are smaller individual components of inventory that do not represent the larger inventory picture. Inventory turnover is calculated as the ratio of the cost of goods sold for the period (usually yearly) to the actual or standard cost of the average inventory in stock (usually determined quarterly).

51. C: The best answer is "c." The item master file should contain all or most of the information the new manager needs to become familiar with the product being manufactured. The item master data file is a record of all of the information about a particular part, including physical, ordering, costing, design, fabrication, and planning information along with associated policies and techniques. Both static information and dynamic information are included. Specific examples of data kept in the item master file are: part description, storage location(s), primary and secondary units of measure along with conversion factors, manufacturing lead time, balance on hand, and quantity allocated.

How to Overcome Test Anxiety

Just the thought of taking a test is enough to make most people a little nervous. A test is an important event that can have a long-term impact on your future, so it's important to take it seriously and it's natural to feel anxious about performing well. But just because anxiety is normal, that doesn't mean that it's helpful in test taking, or that you should simply accept it as part of your life. Anxiety can have a variety of effects. These effects can be mild, like making you feel slightly nervous, or severe, like blocking your ability to focus or remember even a simple detail.

If you experience test anxiety—whether severe or mild—it's important to know how to beat it. To discover this, first you need to understand what causes test anxiety.

Causes of Test Anxiety

While we often think of anxiety as an uncontrollable emotional state, it can actually be caused by simple, practical things. One of the most common causes of test anxiety is that a person does not feel adequately prepared for their test. This feeling can be the result of many different issues such as poor study habits or lack of organization, but the most common culprit is time management. Starting to study too late, failing to organize your study time to cover all of the material, or being distracted while you study will mean that you're not well prepared for the test. This may lead to cramming the night before, which will cause you to be physically and mentally exhausted for the test. Poor time management also contributes to feelings of stress, fear, and hopelessness as you realize you are not well prepared but don't know what to do about it.

Other times, test anxiety is not related to your preparation for the test but comes from unresolved fear. This may be a past failure on a test, or poor performance on tests in general. It may come from comparing yourself to others who seem to be performing better or from the stress of living up to expectations. Anxiety may be driven by fears of the future—how failure on this test would affect your educational and career goals. These fears are often completely irrational, but they can still negatively impact your test performance.

Elements of Test Anxiety

As mentioned earlier, test anxiety is considered to be an emotional state, but it has physical and mental components as well. Sometimes you may not even realize that you are suffering from test anxiety until you notice the physical symptoms. These can include trembling hands, rapid heartbeat, sweating, nausea, and tense muscles. Extreme anxiety may lead to fainting or vomiting. Obviously, any of these symptoms can have a negative impact on testing. It is important to recognize them as soon as they begin to occur so that you can address the problem before it damages your performance.

The mental components of test anxiety include trouble focusing and inability to remember learned information. During a test, your mind is on high alert, which can help you recall information and stay focused for an extended period of time. However, anxiety interferes with your mind's natural processes, causing you to blank out, even on the questions you know well. The strain of testing during anxiety makes it difficult to stay focused, especially on a test that may take several hours. Extreme anxiety can take a huge mental toll, making it difficult not only to recall test information but even to understand the test questions or pull your thoughts together.

Effects of Test Anxiety

Test anxiety is like a disease—if left untreated, it will get progressively worse. Anxiety leads to poor performance, and this reinforces the feelings of fear and failure, which in turn lead to poor performances on subsequent tests. It can grow from a mild nervousness to a crippling condition. If allowed to progress, test anxiety can have a big impact on your schooling, and consequently on your future.

Test anxiety can spread to other parts of your life. Anxiety on tests can become anxiety in any stressful situation, and blanking on a test can turn into panicking in a job situation. But fortunately, you don't have to let anxiety rule your testing and determine your grades. There are a number of relatively simple steps you can take to move past anxiety and function normally on a test and in the rest of life.

Physical Steps for Beating Test Anxiety

While test anxiety is a serious problem, the good news is that it can be overcome. It doesn't have to control your ability to think and remember information. While it may take time, you can begin taking steps today to beat anxiety.

Just as your first hint that you may be struggling with anxiety comes from the physical symptoms, the first step to treating it is also physical. Rest is crucial for having a clear, strong mind. If you are tired, it is much easier to give in to anxiety. But if you establish good sleep habits, your body and mind will be ready to perform optimally, without the strain of exhaustion. Additionally, sleeping well helps you to retain information better, so you're more likely to recall the answers when you see the test questions.

Getting good sleep means more than going to bed on time. It's important to allow your brain time to relax. Take study breaks from time to time so it doesn't get overworked, and don't study right before bed. Take time to rest your mind before trying to rest your body, or you may find it difficult to fall asleep.

Along with sleep, other aspects of physical health are important in preparing for a test. Good nutrition is vital for good brain function. Sugary foods and drinks may give a burst of energy but this burst is followed by a crash, both physically and emotionally. Instead, fuel your body with protein and vitamin-rich foods.

Also, drink plenty of water. Dehydration can lead to headaches and exhaustion, especially if your brain is already under stress from the rigors of the test. Particularly if your test is a long one, drink water during the breaks. And if possible, take an energy-boosting snack to eat between sections.

Along with sleep and diet, a third important part of physical health is exercise. Maintaining a steady workout schedule is helpful, but even taking 5-minute study breaks to walk can help get your blood pumping faster and clear your head. Exercise also releases endorphins, which contribute to a positive feeling and can help combat test anxiety.

When you nurture your physical health, you are also contributing to your mental health. If your body is healthy, your mind is much more likely to be healthy as well. So take time to rest, nourish your body with healthy food and water, and get moving as much as possible. Taking these physical steps will make you stronger and more able to take the mental steps necessary to overcome test anxiety.

Mental Steps for Beating Test Anxiety

Working on the mental side of test anxiety can be more challenging, but as with the physical side, there are clear steps you can take to overcome it. As mentioned earlier, test anxiety often stems from lack of preparation, so the obvious solution is to prepare for the test. Effective studying may be the most important weapon you have for beating test anxiety, but you can and should employ several other mental tools to combat fear.

First, boost your confidence by reminding yourself of past success—tests or projects that you aced. If you're putting as much effort into preparing for this test as you did for those, there's no reason you should expect to fail here. Work hard to prepare; then trust your preparation.

Second, surround yourself with encouraging people. It can be helpful to find a study group, but be sure that the people you're around will encourage a positive attitude. If you spend time with others who are anxious or cynical, this will only contribute to your own anxiety. Look for others who are motivated to study hard from a desire to succeed, not from a fear of failure.

Third, reward yourself. A test is physically and mentally tiring, even without anxiety, and it can be helpful to have something to look forward to. Plan an activity following the test, regardless of the outcome, such as going to a movie or getting ice cream.

When you are taking the test, if you find yourself beginning to feel anxious, remind yourself that you know the material. Visualize successfully completing the test. Then take a few deep, relaxing breaths and return to it. Work through the questions carefully but with confidence, knowing that you are capable of succeeding.

Developing a healthy mental approach to test taking will also aid in other areas of life. Test anxiety affects more than just the actual test—it can be damaging to your mental health and even contribute to depression. It's important to beat test anxiety before it becomes a problem for more than testing.

Study Strategy

Being prepared for the test is necessary to combat anxiety, but what does being prepared look like? You may study for hours on end and still not feel prepared. What you need is a strategy for test prep. The next few pages outline our recommended steps to help you plan out and conquer the challenge of preparation.

Step 1: Scope Out the Test

Learn everything you can about the format (multiple choice, essay, etc.) and what will be on the test. Gather any study materials, course outlines, or sample exams that may be available. Not only will this help you to prepare, but knowing what to expect can help to alleviate test anxiety.

Step 2: Map Out the Material

Look through the textbook or study guide and make note of how many chapters or sections it has. Then divide these over the time you have. For example, if a book has 15 chapters and you have five days to study, you need to cover three chapters each day. Even better, if you have the time, leave an extra day at the end for overall review after you have gone through the material in depth.

If time is limited, you may need to prioritize the material. Look through it and make note of which sections you think you already have a good grasp on, and which need review. While you are studying, skim quickly through the familiar sections and take more time on the challenging parts.

Write out your plan so you don't get lost as you go. Having a written plan also helps you feel more in control of the study, so anxiety is less likely to arise from feeling overwhelmed at the amount to cover.

Step 3: Gather Your Tools

Decide what study method works best for you. Do you prefer to highlight in the book as you study and then go back over the highlighted portions? Or do you type out notes of the important information? Or is it helpful to make flashcards that you can carry with you? Assemble the pens, index cards, highlighters, post-it notes, and any other materials you may need so you won't be distracted by getting up to find things while you study.

If you're having a hard time retaining the information or organizing your notes, experiment with different methods. For example, try color-coding by subject with colored pens, highlighters, or post-it notes. If you learn better by hearing, try recording yourself reading your notes so you can listen while in the car, working out, or simply sitting at your desk. Ask a friend to quiz you from your flashcards, or try teaching someone the material to solidify it in your mind.

Step 4: Create Your Environment

It's important to avoid distractions while you study. This includes both the obvious distractions like visitors and the subtle distractions like an uncomfortable chair (or a too-comfortable couch that makes you want to fall asleep). Set up the best study environment possible: good lighting and a comfortable work area. If background music helps you focus, you may want to turn it on, but otherwise keep the room quiet. If you are using a computer to take notes, be sure you don't have any other windows open, especially applications like social media, games, or anything else that could distract you. Silence your phone and turn off notifications. Be sure to keep water close by so you stay hydrated while you study (but avoid unhealthy drinks and snacks).

Also, take into account the best time of day to study. Are you freshest first thing in the morning? Try to set aside some time then to work through the material. Is your mind clearer in the afternoon or evening? Schedule your study session then. Another method is to study at the same time of day that you will take the test, so that your brain gets used to working on the material at that time and will be ready to focus at test time.

Step 5: Study!

Once you have done all the study preparation, it's time to settle into the actual studying. Sit down, take a few moments to settle your mind so you can focus, and begin to follow your study plan. Don't give in to distractions or let yourself procrastinate. This is your time to prepare so you'll be ready to fearlessly approach the test. Make the most of the time and stay focused.

Of course, you don't want to burn out. If you study too long you may find that you're not retaining the information very well. Take regular study breaks. For example, taking five minutes out of every hour to walk briskly, breathing deeply and swinging your arms, can help your mind stay fresh.

As you get to the end of each chapter or section, it's a good idea to do a quick review. Remind yourself of what you learned and work on any difficult parts. When you feel that you've mastered the material, move on to the next part. At the end of your study session, briefly skim through your notes again.

But while review is helpful, cramming last minute is NOT. If at all possible, work ahead so that you won't need to fit all your study into the last day. Cramming overloads your brain with more information than it can process and retain, and your tired mind may struggle to recall even previously learned information when it is overwhelmed with last-minute study. Also, the urgent nature of cramming and the stress placed on your brain contribute to anxiety. You'll be more likely to go to the test feeling unprepared and having trouble thinking clearly.

So don't cram, and don't stay up late before the test, even just to review your notes at a leisurely pace. Your brain needs rest more than it needs to go over the information again. In fact, plan to finish your studies by noon or early afternoon the day before the test. Give your brain the rest of the day to relax or focus on other things, and get a good night's sleep. Then you will be fresh for the test and better able to recall what you've studied.

Step 6: Take a Practice Test

Many courses offer sample tests, either online or in the study materials. This is an excellent resource to check whether you have mastered the material, as well as to prepare for the test format and environment.

Check the test format ahead of time: the number of questions, the type (multiple choice, free response, etc.), and the time limit. Then create a plan for working through them. For example, if you have 30 minutes to take a 60-question test, your limit is 30 seconds per question. Spend less time on the questions you know well so that you can take more time on the difficult ones.

If you have time to take several practice tests, take the first one open book, with no time limit. Work through the questions at your own pace and make sure you fully understand them. Gradually work up to taking a test under test conditions: sit at a desk with all study materials put away and set a timer. Pace yourself to make sure you finish the test with time to spare and go back to check your answers if you have time.

After each test, check your answers. On the questions you missed, be sure you understand why you missed them. Did you misread the question (tests can use tricky wording)? Did you forget the information? Or was it something you hadn't learned? Go back and study any shaky areas that the practice tests reveal.

Taking these tests not only helps with your grade, but also aids in combating test anxiety. If you're already used to the test conditions, you're less likely to worry about it, and working through tests until you're scoring well gives you a confidence boost. Go through the practice tests until you feel comfortable, and then you can go into the test knowing that you're ready for it.

Test Tips

On test day, you should be confident, knowing that you've prepared well and are ready to answer the questions. But aside from preparation, there are several test day strategies you can employ to maximize your performance.

First, as stated before, get a good night's sleep the night before the test (and for several nights before that, if possible). Go into the test with a fresh, alert mind rather than staying up late to study.

Try not to change too much about your normal routine on the day of the test. It's important to eat a nutritious breakfast, but if you normally don't eat breakfast at all, consider eating just a protein bar. If you're a coffee drinker, go ahead and have your normal coffee. Just make sure you time it so that the caffeine doesn't wear off right in the middle of your test. Avoid sugary beverages, and drink enough water to stay hydrated but not so much that you need a restroom break 10 minutes into the test. If your test isn't first thing in the morning, consider going for a walk or doing a light workout before the test to get your blood flowing.

Allow yourself enough time to get ready, and leave for the test with plenty of time to spare so you won't have the anxiety of scrambling to arrive in time. Another reason to be early is to select a good seat. It's helpful to sit away from doors and windows, which can be distracting. Find a good seat, get out your supplies, and settle your mind before the test begins.

When the test begins, start by going over the instructions carefully, even if you already know what to expect. Make sure you avoid any careless mistakes by following the directions.

Then begin working through the questions, pacing yourself as you've practiced. If you're not sure on an answer, don't spend too much time on it, and don't let it shake your confidence. Either skip it and come back later, or eliminate as many wrong answers as possible and guess among the remaining ones. Don't dwell on these questions as you continue—put them out of your mind and focus on what lies ahead.

Be sure to read all of the answer choices, even if you're sure the first one is the right answer. Sometimes you'll find a better one if you keep reading. But don't second-guess yourself if you do immediately know the answer. Your gut instinct is usually right. Don't let test anxiety rob you of the information you know.

If you have time at the end of the test (and if the test format allows), go back and review your answers. Be cautious about changing any, since your first instinct tends to be correct, but make sure you didn't misread any of the questions or accidentally mark the wrong answer choice. Look over any you skipped and make an educated guess.

At the end, leave the test feeling confident. You've done your best, so don't waste time worrying about your performance or wishing you could change anything. Instead, celebrate the successful completion of this test. And finally, use this test to learn how to deal with anxiety even better next time.

Review Video: Test Anxiety
Visit mometrix.com/academy and enter code: 100340

Important Qualification

Not all anxiety is created equal. If your test anxiety is causing major issues in your life beyond the classroom or testing center, or if you are experiencing troubling physical symptoms related to your anxiety, it may be a sign of a serious physiological or psychological condition. If this sounds like your situation, we strongly encourage you to seek professional help.

Online Resources

Due to our efforts to try to keep this book to a manageable length, we've created a link that will give you access to all of your online resources:

mometrix.com/resources719/cpimdsp

It's Your Moment, Let's Celebrate It!

Share your story @mometrixtestpreparation